CHALK TALK

E-ADVICE FROM JONAS CHALK

LEGENDARY COLLEGE TEACHER

DONNA M. QUALTERS
MIRIAM ROSALYN DIAMOND

NEW FORUMS PRESS INC.
Stillwater, Okla. U.S.A.

NEW FORUMS PRESS INC.

Published in the United States of America
by New Forums Press, Inc.
1018 S. Lewis St.
Stillwater, OK 74074
www.newforums.com

Library of Congress Cataloging-in-Publication Data Pending

This book may be ordered in bulk quantities at discount from
New Forums Press, Inc., P.O. Box 876, Stillwater, OK 74076
[Federal I.D. No. 73 1123239]. Printed in the United States of
America.

International Standard Book Number: 1-58107-085-3

Acknowledgements

Jonas would like to thank the following people for their contributions to this work:

- Deans Alan Soyster and James Stellar for their visionary initiation of the collaboration between Northeastern's Colleges of Arts and Science and Engineering.

- Members of the General Electric Learning Excellence Initiative for their support of the Master Teachers program.

- David Thompkins for his direction in grant proposal and preparation.

- Assistant Dean David Navick for his assiduous data collection and analysis.

- Jonas team members Dr. David Hirsch, Professor Nathan Israeloff, Professor Ira Krull, Laurie Poklop, Professor Timothy Sage, and Professor Darien Wood for their wisdom and insights.

- Professor Beverly Jaeger and Dr. Richard Harris for sharing their resourcefulness and expertise.

- Alicia Russell for her role in developing an electronic education development vision. Katelyn O'Brien and Emily Marsden for seeing that the vision reach fruition.

- Professor Elise Dallimore and graduate assistant Melissa Plumb for their efforts in making educational research available to scientists and engineers.

- Cynthia Sanders for her talent and insight in facilitating the final edits and Carree Michel for assistance in exploring web sites.

- The Jonas Chalk column readers who contributed their questions and tips to sustain and continue discussions on effective teaching.

- The many students who motivated us to write these columns and who continue to inspire faculty to become better teachers.

Finally, Jonas would like to acknowledge the on-going support, wisdom and insight of his soul mate, Dusty Chalk. Behind every great legend, there's an even greater goddess!

TABLE OF CONTENTS

Dedication

This book is dedicated to:

- *Mark Dullea and Brett and Meghan Qualters*

- *The Diamonds, the Grosses, the Malkas, and the Werthimers*

who have provided us with their advice and guidance.

Chapter 1

Dear Jonas: Why an E-Advice Column?

Donna M. Qualters

Higher education is notoriously slow to change. The adoption of new ideas often takes years to achieve as they wind their way through a complex governance system. This dynamic is prevalent in the practices of higher education, especially in the area of classroom teaching. Changing teaching practices, whether it is the introduction of active learning, the use of technology, or learning classroom assessment techniques, is often seen as an impossible task. Why? One reason is that topics such as learning theory, educational philosophy, and teaching methodology are usually not part of the extensive education that is required to be a college professor. When faculty begin their teaching careers without this background, they often approach teaching in one of two ways: they either teach the way they were taught or teach the way that best reflects their personal learning style. Consciously or unconsciously, repeated unexamined practice becomes their teaching philosophy and drives their methodology.

This helps to explain why many higher education classrooms today are still very traditional despite the extensive research devoted to best teaching and learning practices. As you peek into today's classes, you see the professor lecturing and writing on the board, students taking notes, and a few tests and final paper determining the grade. When these methods do not work, trained researchers who use meticulous protocols in the research arena of their professional life resort to a random trial-and-error approach to figure out what to do in the classroom.

The problem for those interested in changing teaching practice is how to engage faculty and get them to change old habits in an informed way – in other words, to have faculty examine what they do in the classroom in light of current research and then actually make a change.

That was the challenge to the Northeastern University Master Teaching Team. The College of Engineering in partnership with the College of Arts and Sciences at Northeastern University in Boston, Massachusetts, received a three-year grant from the General Electric Learning Excellence Fund to improve the learning outcomes and the learning experience of engineering students, especially freshmen. This grant allowed us to form the Master Teaching Team comprised of faculty from the School of Engineering and the School of Arts and Science, along with members of the Center for Effective University Teaching (CEUT) and the Educational Technology Center (Ed Tech). An interdisciplinary subset of this group became the Instructional Development Group and was charged with designing a faculty development plan that would improve teaching across disciplinary boundaries and introduce new teaching methods that would be appropriate to a wide variety of disciplines – a formidable task!

We did have some roadmaps from the organizational change literature to guide us in this endeavor. Seminal literature such as Chin and Benne (1969) developed strategies and models that are particularly adaptable to help faculty develop as teachers. They identified strategies that form the framework of models to engage groups in the change process. One of the strategies, called the Normative/Re-educative Approach, engages participants in the development process by using "real problems" and then having participants actively involved in the decision-making process on how to design solutions for these problems. Today we call this problem based learning (PBL). In PBL groups are presented with contextual situations and asked to define the problem, decide what skills and resources are necessary to investigate the problem, and then pose possible solutions (Duch, Groh, and Allen, 2001). In many ways this is what faculty must do. They are confronted with real muddy problems in the context of their class that they must address. In essence, like their students, they must define what the problem is, what do they already know about it, what do they not know, where can they find the information, and most importantly what can they do.

Different models have emerged from this strategy that have been applied to the field of faculty development. The product-oriented model has faculty identifying the problem but calling on "expert help" to provide a solution. For example, a faculty member who is concerned about lack of response in class discussions because no one has done the reading ahead will look for a workshop on encouraging students to do assignments ahead of time. The second approach, the prescription-oriented model also calls for expert outside help, but in this model faculty cannot identify the cause and "the expert" is engaged to assist in problem definition. An example of this model would be a department's faculty who are concerned about attrition rates in their major but are not sure why students are dropping out. They would then seek advice from colleagues in enrollment management to help them figure out the parameters of the problem before designing a solution. In the third approach, the process-oriented model, experts work with the department to provide necessary skills needed to change. Asking a member of the Assessment Center to help a department develop a learning assessment model for the major would exemplify this model. Finally, the problem-oriented model provides a collaborative process with faculty and experts *working together* to diagnose and propose strategies. The important point of this model is that it leaves the final decision on how to proceed (or not) to the faculty.

In choosing a strategy/model to help faculty improve their classroom teaching we have to remember that in higher education we are not changing systems so much as changing individuals in the system. Individualism has been, and continues to be, a characteristic of faculty identity from the very beginning of the professorate in higher education (Rostovsky, 1990). This entrepreneurial attitude often creates individuals who pursue their own agendas in their own way. Therefore, faculty who perceive they are good teachers and have conflicting responsibilities and priorities in the area of research and service often do not have the inclination to pursue teaching development activities.

The perception of how good their teaching is often comes from assumptions they have formed through many years of teaching practice. But as Angelo (1997) reminds us, much of what is viewed as practice in higher education is actually *unexamined* assumptions. Therefore, in order to create change in teaching behaviors there must be a way to have faculty think about these unexamined assumptions that form the basis of their practice and their teaching decisions. Literature on intentional change outlines some common elements necessary in programs to create change. To change individuals there must be an examination of practice, a surfacing of assumptions, an examination of the validity of assumptions, real suggestions from practitioners and support for those going through the change process (Robertson, 1988; Schon, 1987, Wenger 1998, Qualters, 2000).

Prochaska and DiClemente (1986) proposed a model that outlined this process of change – a model that the GE Master Teaching Team used to develop an approach that would engage faculty in the process of looking at their own practice

---

and considering improvements in teaching and learning. Individual change occurs along a continuum (see figure 1) and, depending on a faculty member's placement on the continuum, different interventions are needed. As we said before, faculty who have been teaching for many years and who are content in their classroom are not likely to seek anything new and different unless they can be convinced that there is some benefit to doing so; these individuals would fall in the pre-contemplative category. Being pre-contemplative also means that individuals in this category, who make up a large portion of any faculty, probably would not utilize more traditional venues such as workshops, seminars, or brown bag lunches.

Any activity devised to meet the above criteria would need to be time-efficient and easy to do; cost-efficient but available to a large number of faculty; cover as many individuals as possible on the change continuum; provide strategies and alternatives in an explicit way but with enough options to allow the faculty member to make the final decision; provide insight to get faculty to think about their own exam-

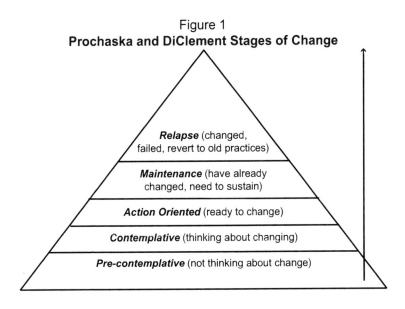

Figure 1
Prochaska and DiClement Stages of Change

Relapse (changed, failed, revert to old practices)

Maintenance (have already changed, need to sustain)

Action Oriented (ready to change)

Contemplative (thinking about changing)

Pre-contemplative (not thinking about change)

ined assumptions; be collegial and allow a partnership to develop between the team and the faculty in improving teaching; and lastly, share some of the literature on teaching and learning that would inform faculty as they design environments to maximize student-learning.

Thus was born *JONAS CHALK: CHALK TALK*. This electronic teaching advice column, written collaboratively by the members of the Instructional Development Group, met all the above criteria. Via e-mail, faculty on our distribution list received a clearly identified Jonas column weekly. The columns contained a common "real" problem in teaching that faculty from any discipline and teaching any group of students might encounter. Jonas then would outline the issues in the problem, identify resources and then suggest possible solutions, always providing a number of options from different discipline perspectives which different team members themselves used to address the problem. These columns were kept short and identified the teaching dilemma in the subject line. Faculty could quickly open the e-mail, scan it, and then save it for future reference or view password protected the archived columns on our GE Master Teaching Team website. This approach gave faculty a number of different techniques from different disciplines to consider. Jonas also provided some informative references for faculty who wanted to explore the topic further and each column had a "Quick Tip" at the end that suggested an activity that could easily be implemented immediately in the very next class they were heading off to teach. The cost to the team involved their time and the establishment of the electronic format and archive. Faculty who read the column also had the opportunity to anonymously pose their own teaching dilemmas to Jonas to get some help either identifying the problem, or getting multiple solutions to an already identified problem.

Jonas began with faculty from engineering, mathematics, physics, chemistry, and the Center for Effective University Teaching (CEUT) sitting down and asking ourselves what were *our* teaching dilemmas, what were *our* challenges in the classroom – in other words examining our own practice. Many of our team were either nominated for, or had been winners of, the Northeastern University Excellence in Teaching award; yet, as you will see in subsequent chapters we were all struggling with very common teaching challenges. This discussion led to our first column on "Lost Students" (see chapter 3). The initial discussion also generated a number of questions for future columns as we listened and responded to each other. The more we talked together across disciplines, the more we realized that, while there are some discipline specific areas, a great deal of what the physics professors were trying to figure out in class were the same issues that the math, chemistry, and engineering professors were also struggling with in the classroom.

As we began to conceive *Jonas*, a number of decisions were made that reflected a collaborative vision of education and formed the basis of the columns. We decided very early not to deal with issues of technology in isolation. We all felt that there was a danger of technology driving the teaching rather than teaching integrating technology where appropriate; that is why there is no chapter in this volume on Teaching with Technology. Rather you will find columns sprinkled throughout the chapters that address the use of technology in ways that help teachers achieve their learning objectives by integrating the technology. Conversely, we decided to devote separate columns to working with teaching assistants (TAs). While many TAs address the same situations in the classroom that the teaching faculty do, they also face supervisory and relationship issues. Faculty, who oversee and mentor TAs, need to think about these supervisory issues to provide an effective classroom environment for everyone. Lastly, we saw the persona of *Jonas* as a colleague; granted, a rather knowledgeable colleague with a command of the teaching and learning literature, but someone who suggested, posed questions, gave both sides of issues, and presented multiple perspectives. *Jonas* was never anyone who told faculty what to do. Instead, this persona became someone faculty could challenge as some of our readers did. However the challenges were not viewed as confrontational by the *Jonas* team. Instead we found that by responding to reader letters the ensuing column always took the teaching conversation to a deeper level. *Jonas* never defended his ideas, but simply laid out in more depth WHY he chose to answer questions the way he did. Reader responses also allowed us to widen our own perspective and better understand our readers' perspectives and challenges.

After running weekly columns for five quarters, we surveyed our targeted readership of approximately 50 faculty and teaching assistants to get their feedback on the usefulness of *Jonas* in changing classroom practices and on getting pre-contemplative faculty to think about changing their practice – the first crucial step in the change continuum. Surveys were sent on-line as part of the *Jonas* column, and paper versions were handed out at luncheon for engineering and arts and science faculty who teach engineering students. Our hope was to also find out how many of our potential participants were actually aware of and/or reading *Jonas*. Our survey generated a 50% return rate from all the disciplines involved in the project and included members of the math, engineering, physics, and chemistry faculty. Respondents ranged from full professors with over 20 years of teaching experience to lecturers and teaching assistants with only a few years of experience.

Of the respondents, 96% were familiar with the column and 92% had actually visited the archived *Jonas* web site. 92% found *Jonas* helpful, 59% had spoken to another colleague about their teaching because of a Chalk Talk column, but most impressive was the fact that 92% had thought about their teaching practices and tried at least one new idea.

Faculty respondent comments showed that they were reflecting and thinking about their practice and choosing to try one or two ideas that *Jonas* had presented. One faculty member told us "(*Jonas*) helped me recognize some of the philosophies I hold and the techniques I use." The concept of reflection was often raised: *Jonas* "helped me think about things," "helped me deal and think about questions from students and their problems," "caused me to consider how I do things and possible techniques I can try," "cause one to reflect on one's own teaching and what one could do better to improve teaching, how to interact better with students and how to be more effective as a communicator and teacher." It would appear that *Jonas* was doing what we had hoped in the original conception of the idea; help faculty think about their teaching practices. In other words, getting faculty to be contemplative, and then for those who were in the action phase providing a variety of techniques from different disciplines that they could experiment with in their own classes.

Because of the success, our advice column received the Professional Organizational and Development Network in Higher Education's (POD) national Bright Idea Grand Award in 2001 in recognition of the innovation in promoting faculty and instructional development on campus. *Jonas* has also been offered to a wider community. It has become a regular column in the CEUT's teaching newsletter *Teaching Matters* and used with permission by other universities.

The Chalk Talk advice column became an efficient and effective way to raise faculty teaching assumptions, provide space for reflection and generate some practical ideas that allows faculty to become contemplative, the first giant step to creating real change.

Works Cited

Angelo,T. (May, 1997) "The Campus as a Learning Community: Seven Promising Shifts and Seven Powerful Levers" *AAHE Bulletin*, 49: 3-6.

Chin, R., and Kenneth B. (1969). "General Strategies for Effecting Changes in Human Systems." In *The Planning of Change: Second Edition*, edited by W.G.Bennes, K.D. Benne, and R. Chin. New York: Holt Rinehart and Winston.

Duch, B.J.; Groh, S.E.; and Allen, D.E., editors (2001). *The Power of Problem-Based Learning: A Practical "How-To" for Teaching Undergraduate Courses in Any Discipline.* Stylus Publishing, LLC, Sterling, Virginia.

Prochaska, J.O., and DiClemente, C.C., (1986) "Toward a Comprehensive Model of Change," in *Treating Addictive Behavior: Processes of Change*, New York: Plenum Press.

Qualters, D. (May, 2000). "Creating faculty Community." *National Teaching and Learning Forum, 9*(4), 1-4.

Robertson, D. L. (1988). *Self-directed growth*. Muncie, IN: Accelerated Development.

Rosovsky, H. (1990). *The University: An owner's manual.* New York & London: WW. Norton & company.

Schon, D. (1983). *The Reflective Practitioner: How Professionals Think in Action.* New York: Basic Books.

Wenger, E. (1998). *Communities of Practice: Learning, Meaning, and Identity.* Cambridge, UK: Cambridge University Press.

Chapter 2

Becoming Jonas: Reflections from the Team

Master Teaching Team

Who is Jonas Chalk? That question was raised in the minds of readers as Jonas columns began to appear in their e-mail week after week. At one time or other, every member of the team has been approached by colleagues and declared to be Jonas. Interestingly, in spite of how knowledgeable and skillful Jonas seemed to be, no one guessed he might be the result of a team effort. Readers preferred to believe that the "voice" of Jonas was an individual. In truth, Jonas is a unique individual; he is a wonderful blend of all participants' voices. Readers got a glimpse of Sue's enthusiasm, Jackie's leadership and attention to detail, Dave's sense of humor, Tom's clear insightful thinking, Rick's passion about freshmen, Miriam's wonderful teaching tips, and Donna's breadth of experience. Yet it was not always that effortless. In surveying the Master Teaching team we found an interesting story of how we "became Jonas Chalk".

Even the team is not sure how Jonas first came about. Two and one-half years later, we struggled to recollect the details of Jonas's birth; stories of who conceived the idea and how the name was chosen differ, depending on whom you ask. But what was perfectly clear to everyone was the purpose of creating the e-advice column. This team was charged with helping their peers become better teachers and they wanted to reach as many colleagues as possible in a way that would be practical, useful and helpful. As one team member said, "We wanted share some best practices with instructors". Our targeted group of potential readers was very diverse. They were faculty and teaching assistants from engineering, mathematics, chemistry, and physics. They varied in age and rank from first year graduate teaching assistants to faculty who had been at the university for over 30 years. In truth, their knowledge of, and interest in, teaching improvement was very different and we wanted to reach *all* professors, not just those already committed to teaching excellence. That common motivation and desire for excellence sustained us in the early phases of this project.

Becoming Jonas was a year-long process, and not always an easy one. Like any group coming together, we went through the stages of group development as we negotiated our way with each other and with finding a "voice" for Jonas. The core team for Jonas was comprised of four men and five women who agreed to meet weekly for an hour. We were from four different academic disciplines as well as the Center for Effective University Teaching and the Educational Technology Center. Many were university wide teaching award nominees or winners, an intimidating group from the demographic outline! Team members frankly were unsure about how this effort would proceed:

> I was uncertain, but curious, about the members from different disciplines. I didn't know how they did things in their departments and how they regarded the students and what they thought of (my) department.

> I wanted to wear my chemical protection suit …but my gut said 'no, take a chance'. I think we all started

with preconceived notions, perhaps me more than others.

But embedded in this uncertainty and assumptions was also an element of curiosity and an excitement about having the opportunity to work with others across the University; learning from excellent teachers; having a place to share concerns that we found we more common than we thought; and just exploring how other disciplines envisioned and practiced the art of teaching. Once the decision was made to craft an advice column we all agreed to give it a try.

Our first task was deciding how to get questions to answer, and then to define a process for answering them. We started talking initially about our own challenges in the classroom and soon found that many of us were having the same concerns. We all struggled with how to get students engaged in the class, what do to when no one answered your questions, how to respond to student excuses and so the questions seemed to write themselves. We soon realized it would take time, knowledge, and experience to comprehensively answer these questions, but as the questions surfaced we found ourselves saying, "This is what I do," "I always do this," "Have you ever tried this?" Collectively, we had a lot of ideas and tips and that our experience was quite extensive. Thus evolved the system of constructing a group question at our meeting, and then soliciting a volunteer to be the lead writer. The writer would draft an answer and bring it to the following meeting to have the group discuss everything from content, to style, to grammar.

The first couple of months of meetings were very different from what occurs today. Initially preparing Jonas columns was only part of a larger meeting because the team was still problem solving a variety of different approaches to faculty development. In addition, we had not yet established rapport, and were self-conscious about bringing our teaching out of the classroom and into a space where it could be scrutinized by others. The words most often used to describe those early days were "business-like," "serious," "short and focused." As one contributor put it:

> I think that in the first meetings where we discussed columns in person, the draft writer was somewhat tentative about criticism. The draft writer was concerned that the column would not be up to par and that he/she did not know the subject enough to have become that week's expert on the topic. The discussions were always cordial and constructive, and everyone always polite...

If you have ever experienced a party where invitees are unfamiliar with each other, then you have a good understanding of our first round of meetings. Discussions were polite and superficial, drafts of answers were fairly short, criticism was either offered very gently or defensively and for the most part, in a serious, tentative manner so as not to hurt anyone's feelings.

The writer's feelings too, were very different in the beginning: "At the start, I felt that I had to circulate a complete and essentially final version," or "When I was initially drafting a Jonas column, my confidence level wasn't high enough to feel qualified to write this," to "I worked very long and hard to write, research, rewrite, with a lot of trepidation about having others see my work and change it." Inherent in these remarks was the impression that as faculty they had to be the expert. If their peers were going to review this, they better know what they were talking about and be able to defend their writing.

Today a Jonas meeting is more reminiscent of a family barbeque than a cocktail party. We are familiar with each other, comfortable with our styles, and accepting of those things we cannot change about our team. As one team member put it:

Probably the principal difference is that we all are more open and any defensiveness has evaporated (and) been replaced by mutual respect and engaging repartee. We have realized and trust that we all operate from the same basic value [or have evolved to them], we want our students to be successful and there are things that we, as teachers, can do to facilitate this success.

In talking about our current get togethers, the adjectives most often used were 'fun,' 'relaxing,' or 'comfortable'– not common words when discussing academic meetings. This positive feeling about the culture of the Jonas team does not rule out discussion or even conflict. The difference today is the way criticism is viewed and handled.

I know that, if I say something incorrectly or something that's plain dumb, I will be challenged – not in a degrading way, probably in a humorous way from a challenger with a broad smile and sparkling eyes.

Now I still work on the research and writing, but I don't worry about comments and criticism, I know it quickly becomes everyone's work, and I am glad that it becomes 'Jonas' property, not me.

Jonas is "our" column now; one member of the team refers to the team as his "fellow Brothers and Sisters Jonas". As we became more comfortable discussing the issues, readers appeared to be more comfortable replying and submitting their own questions. There is some concern that we may be worrying our columns too much, or have made our columns more politically correct than necessary, but that may be because we are now engaging the problem at deeper levels and trying to cover all angles of the issue in our reply, rather than simply providing a response. We want our readers to develop the same conscientiousness about teaching and learning that we have. So while a question may be about how to construct a multiple choice test, the answer often involves awareness of learning styles, understanding and setting measurable objectives and responding to situations that occur during the testing.

This freedom and lack of ego that has developed as we became Jonas has transformed our team into individuals who now think much more deeply about teaching and learning in a comfortable environment. We may have started off with writing Jonas as an interesting idea, but it has evolved into the scholarship of teaching for team members. We now create columns that are based on the literature and in reflected practice. Our discussions are more authentic and grounded in practice. We challenge now, but with an eye to improving "our" column and "our" teaching.

> Now the issues that we deal with are more complex, and so the 'answers aren't easy.' Also knowing that others are going to insert material to cover any point that isn't thoroughly covered makes me think harder about responding to every conceivable issue that's related to the question.

Being Jonas has made us individually and collectively more reflective, thoughtful, and scholarly about what we teach and how we teach. Our focus has shifted from just sharing best practices to really examining the educational process and interconnection of teaching and learning. We talk more about learning and assessment now as well as teaching methodology and tips. These more intense discussions often create more intense conflict but:

> ...it is not negative conflict. On the contrary, it is constructive conflict that leads to new ideas and new approaches to teaching.

Being Jonas has had an effect on the team as teachers as well. You cannot be involved in an experience this intense and concentrated without it having an effect on your own practice. While many of us knew what we should be doing (espoused theory) we often were not doing it (theory in practice)! Being Jonas made us examine our own teaching; even teaching that we thought was pretty good to begin with.

> There's also no question but that I am a better teacher as a result of the interactions with 'my Brothers and Sisters Jonas'. Basically my teaching style has not been changed but my syllabus is more complete and useful to students; I'm more attuned to the diversity of learning styles among students in my classes; and I more easily put myself into my students' shoes as I prepare class material.

Understanding that there are many ways to approach teaching, has allowed members of the Jonas team to be more adventuresome in their own classroom.

> It's also made me experiment with new things that my fellow Jonas-ers are talking about. It has 'decalcified' my teaching by motivating me to change things, try new things, take some teaching risks.

> As part of Jonas, ...I essentially feel obligated to do what Jonas suggests in all of his columns, and so, I do!"

Becoming Jonas also created a larger sense of connection with the university as a whole. Jonas team members began to feel part of a larger community than just their disciplines. We developed a sense of how other departments worked, what was going on in administrative areas, making members feel "more a part of the Northeastern University community". Being Jonas has allowed for continued professional growth for team members as well. While writing the Jonas column was a faculty development intervention for our colleagues, being on the Jonas team became a faculty development activity in and of itself.

> …being Jonas has made me see the importance of 'talking about teaching' and I value this time, and this activity over going to a conference of workshop. It is ongoing, growing and affects change in the way I think, it challenges me, makes me think and question things I thought I knew. So I want to keep 'being Jonas' for me, and I hope that it is having an effect on others. It seems to affect us all.

Being Jonas has created a group of diverse committed faculty, who have grown and developed as teachers, as advisors, as colleagues. The continued growth in our own knowledge base, our awareness of the complexity of teaching, our increasing familiarity with the literature of teaching and learning has produced the "voice" of Jonas; a voice that is united in purpose, humorous and informed in style, caring and compassionate in tone, yet a voice that always calls for excellence in teaching.

We asked our Jonas team members who they felt Jonas was. Their replies show the amalgamation of experiences and expertise that made up this nearly-mythological phenomenon:

> Jonas is this very wise, but not overly pedantic, teaching guru who knows the teaching literature, human nature, and classroom dynamics. He wants to share his knowledge without telling you that his ways are the only ways.

Jonas is partly the conscience of the university teacher. He/she always tells you to be responsible and do the right thing, which is rarely the easy thing. Sometimes Jonas is the kindly old professor who understands your problems and has sage advice to offer. Other times, Jonas is the scholarly professional, who understands the research and the literature of teaching and can bring up appropriate results from controlled studies and statistical analysis.

I think Jonas is a lot like Santa Claus. Even though I know he is fictional, a part of me believes that he really exists. He is the collective spirit of everyone's best intentions toward students and everyone's aspirations to being the best teacher they can be. But Jonas is also human. He recognizes the very real challenges and frustrations faced by faculty, and has developed his expertise only through experience.

Jonas is an interesting fellow with a whole lot of teaching experience. Not only that, he has taught engineering, math, physics, chemistry, and education courses. He's won a number of teaching awards. He's taught large classes and small classes. He has both male and female characteristics and sensibilities. He's taught freshmen through graduate students. Some might think he is possessed of multiple personalities, somehow though, he manages to speak with a single sensible voice. He is well respected by his readers as his commitment to providing quality education clearly shines through his writings; yet he sensitive to the realities of students and classrooms. He's able to integrate education theory, student development theory, and observations to produce practical advice and suggestions.

Jonas is a young, energetic, wise, old, opinionated, open-minded, active reflective teacher.

Jonas is comprised of a number of personalities that have the best interests of teachers (and students) in mind.

Jonas is the memory and future of every teacher who has ever tackled one of the most difficult, rewarding jobs on earth, that of being a teacher.

Jonas now invites you to share in this amazing profession, and hopes that the words and advice that you read in the following pages will enrich your teaching life and that of your students. Who is Jonas? Jonas is all of us!

Chapter 3

Dear Jonas:
Where's the Cafeteria? or What's the Best Way to Reach Freshmen?

Richard Scranton

When a brand new college graduate shows up for the first day at work and asks where the cafeteria is, the supervisor does not say, "Find it yourself; you'll be better for it." Instinctively, employers recognize that this new employee is moving into a new environment and culture and will benefit from guidance and mentoring. They also recognize that this person's productivity and contributions during his or her fourth quarter with the firm will far exceed those that can be reasonably expected during the first quarter. Yet, do we as college instructors plan to treat a brand new first-year student attending his first college course any differently than an upper class student or do we expect first-year students to find the cafeteria on their own? Does a first-year student view class as a "boot camp" experience where only the fittest will move on or as an educationally developmental experience that, as long as s/he does her/his part, will lead to success? Not three months earlier this young person, in all likelihood, was a high school student living at home with her/his parents.

Chickering (1994) suggests that the higher education experience should be examined in three stages: "moving in, moving through and moving on." He notes:

Helping students move into college is far and away our most important responsibility. It is critically important for each student; its consequences for student success and for attrition make it critically important for the institution. Yet, the time, energy, and resources devoted to this transition fall far short of what's needed. The key issues to address are helping students make the transition itself, and helping them develop or discover motivation for learning. (3).

Tinto (1987) notes that new students come to us with different family backgrounds, skills and abilities, prior schooling, expectations, intentions, goals and commitment to the institution, as well as external commitments. He goes on to note that important factors leading to academic and social integration (and therefore retention) into the institution include both formal and informal interactions with faculty, staff and peers. With regard to students who choose to leave a college or university, Tinto concludes:

Institutions of higher education are not unlike other human communities, and the process of educational departure is not substantially different from the other processes of leaving which occur among human communities generally. In both instances, departure mirrors the absence of social and intellectual integration into or membership in community life and of the social support such integration provides. An institution's capacity to retain students is directly related to its ability to reach out and make contact with students and integrate them into the social and intellectual fabric of institutional life. It hinges on the establishment of a healthy, caring educational environment which enables all individuals, not just some, to find a niche in one or more of the many social and intellectual communities of the institution. (180-181)

The marked impact on students of faculty expectations and conduct is highlighted in a recent study by Seymour and Hewitt (1997). They studied science, math, and engineering (S.M.E.) students with SAT scores in mathematics of at least 650 who persevered in their original majors as well as those who chose to switch to non-math, science and engineering majors. They note:

> In one way or another, concerns about teaching, advising, assessment practices and curriculum design, pervade all but seven of the 23 issues represented in our 'iceberg' tables. Thus:
>
> - The rejection of S.M.E. careers or lifestyles is partly a rejection of the role models which S.M.E. faculty and graduate students present to undergraduates.
>
> - S.M.E. faculty are often represented as 'unapproachable' or unavailable for help with either academic or career-planning concerns.
>
> - Students perceive the curve-grading systems widely employed by S.M.E. faculty as reflecting disdain for the worth or potential of most underclassmen. Their presumed purpose is to drive a high proportion of students away, rather than give useful feedback to students on their level of understanding, or conceptual progress.
>
> - Harsh grading systems, which are part of a traditional competitive S.M.E. culture, also preclude or discourage collaborative learning strategies, which many students view as critical to a good understanding of the material, and to a deeper appreciation of the concepts and their application." (34 -35)

The "moving in process" is real. We all go through some version when we begin something new. So do young people who show up on the college campus for the first time. That's why employers of newly graduated employees do not expect the graduates to be as productive as they will be after a year or so.

Many of the first-year students who come to us have never had a roommate before and never washed their own clothes. They've left behind a trusted peer support group and are now evolving to a new one on campus. Most are away from their home environment for an extended time for the first time. More importantly, they must accept the responsibility for making decisions without the direct and immediate influence of an adult. If they oversleep for an 8:00 am class, no one is there to wake them up. If they mention at dinner that they're going out that night, no one is going to ask if their homework is done.

The instructor of a first-year class faces wide diversity in readiness and preparation for that class. In scientific majors all have had a high school physics class – some taught at a very complex level and some not. They come to us from almost as many high schools as there are students in the class and with a high school frame of reference. Many have never seen a syllabus and many have never had grades scaled.

Faculty can contribute both positively and negatively along multiple dimensions of development. We must teach well. However, we also have the obligation to be encouraging coaches, to help students understand and stretch their capabilities. Like it or not, we are role models. Students are acute observers of our behaviors (not just what we do, but how we do it). Are we behaving respectfully, ethically and responsibly? Do we respond in an adult and constructive manner to immature behavior? Are our relationships with our students both inside and outside of class courteous and nurturing? Do we reach out to help those in difficulty or do we avoid helping? Do we demand certain behaviors from our students that we ourselves don't adhere to? Is our response to challenge measured and appropriate, or petty and punitive? When we tell students what we expect from them, do we also tell them what they should expect from us? Should we expect the same level of performance from a freshman as we do from a senior?

In this chapter, Jonas' correspondence tries to raise awareness of these issues and let instructors know how to contribute positively to this moving in process. In short, Jonas reminds faculty teaching first-year students that helping them find the cafeteria is important.

Further Reading

Books

1. Chickering, A. (1994, December). "Empowering Lifelong Self-development," *AAHE Bulletin.*

2. Koch, Andrew K. (2001). *The First-Year Experience in American Higher Education: An Annotated Bibliography.* 3rd Edition. The First-Year Experience Monograph Series, No. 3.

3. Seymour, E. and Hewitt, N. (1997). *Talking About Leaving: Why Undergraduates Leave the Sciences.* Westview Press

4. Tinto, V. (1987,1994). *Leaving College: Rethinking the Causes and Cures of Student Attrition,* Chicago Press

Articles

1. Braxton, John M., and McClendon, Shederick A. (2001-2002). *The Fostering of Social Integration and Retention through*

Institutional Practice. Journal of College Student Retention: Research, Theory & Practice, v3, n1: 57-71.

2.   Gardner, John N. (Fall 2001). *Focusing on the First-Year Student.* Priorities, n17, Fall 2001.

3.   Tinto, Vincent. (1990). *Principles of Effective Retention.* Journal of the Freshman Year Experience, v2, n1: 35-48.

Websites

1.   The First-year Interest Groups (FIGs) Program at Western Washington University http://figs.wwu.edu/

2.   The Hallmarks of Excellence in the First Year of College http://www.brevard.edu/firstyearhallmarks

3.   Standards for Success http://www.s4s.org/

LOST STUDENTS

Dear **Jonas,**

Some of the students in my Calculus 2 class are clearly lost - I can tell from their quizzes, and their blank stares. Still, they don't ask questions in class, they don't come to my office hours, and they don't even come to class sometimes. I don't know what to do. Please help.

Perplexed Professor

Dear **Perplexed,**

I certainly don't have all the answers, but I have some suggestions. Sometimes students get so lost that they essentially give up, even though they don't withdraw and still come to class every now and then. Since your question centers on Calculus 2, I assume you're teaching mostly freshmen. As I'm sure you realize, many freshmen (in transition from high school student to college student) are in need of coaching to learn how to learn and to develop a commitment to learning. Freshmen are often reluctant to speak out in class or feel that they are the only ones who have a question.

You might try a couple of classroom assessment techniques to safely involve them in asking questions. One device is an anonymous one-minute paper. At the end of class, pass out 3x5 cards and ask them to write down anything that is unclear or they have a question about. You can then review the cards and address the most prevalent questions the next class. Another way to get them talking is "concept questions". You can ask a conceptual calculus question and give them a minute to write down the answer, have them turn to a partner and discuss the answer and compile questions they both have and then bring the group back together to discuss the answer. This way they've already talked with someone else and have joint questions so they are probably more willing to participate.

To help avoid student reluctance to seek help in the first place, one colleague insists that all freshmen get a signature on their first homework set from a tutor in the student tutoring office. The idea is that once a student has met the tutors face-to-face and has been received warmly, s/he is more likely to return for help. You could ask that each of your students stop by your office to get your signature too. Welcome them when they visit and use the opportunity to get to know them a little as individuals.

However, once this lost student problem has developed, there are a number of things that you might do. Try mentioning your concerns to your students and then listening to what they have to say. You'll have to create an environment where students can feel free to be candid, be careful not to seem defensive. This can be done on an individual basis or in a group. When individuals perceive that their opinions and feelings are valued, they are likely to become more responsive in future classes. The Center for Effective University Teaching offers a mid-term feedback program that includes a visit to an instructor's class to conduct a confidential discussion about the issues identified with the instructor. Encourage individual students personally to come to your office hours, and if they're still taking quizzes, try writing notes to this effect on the returned papers. You might try to offer a voluntary review session outside of class hours - this type of action sends a strong signal that you are personally committed to their success. If the lost students are engineering students, you can notify the Engineering Student Services Office, and they will try to intervene.

However, if you try all these things, and still get no response, you should realize that, at some point, students have to make their own decisions and take responsibility for their success (or lack thereof). Take care.

Jonas

> **Quick Tip:** For a first assignment have students write a letter about themselves. They can tell you where they are from, hobbies, work experiences and career goals. This will help them understand that you see them as individuals and are interested in who they are, and let you know where they are coming from.

HELPING FRESHMEN GET "UP TO SPEED"

Dear **Jonas:**

I've recently graded and returned the first quiz in my class. This class is for first-year engineering students and, while there were many good grades on the quiz, way too many students did poorly. It was clear from their reactions when I handed the quiz back that many were surprised and demoralized by their poor performance. I spent a lot of time re-explaining how the grading works in my class, that they'd have plenty of opportunities to raise their grades through homework, other quizzes and exams; that didn't seem to help lift their spirits. Also, the quiz obviously showed that many students need help outside of class to get up to speed. What can I tell the struggling students? Where can they find the help they need to do better in my class?

Inquiring Instructor

Dear **Inquiring:**

If you've taught first-year engineering students before, you probably already know that they come from all different backgrounds with different levels of preparation. In addition, they have varying degrees of maturity and self-discipline to deal with this new experience called college. Part of the first

---

year experience is bringing everyone up to a level playing field with respect to academic preparation. For some students, this may be a time when some of what they learn is review from a high school physics or math course; for others, the first year courses will be completely new, and these latter students may struggle to keep up.

There are a number of resources that we can offer to students to help them get up to speed or to give them the support they need to succeed in the first year. An obvious resource is you! You should encourage them to come to your office hours, maybe even explain in class what office hours are about. You could make an early assignment that requires them to come to office hours to get a homework initialed by you; it will let them see that it's not that scary (yes, they may be thinking that), and they might ask a question while they're there. If you have a teaching assistant, you should also let students know that the TA's for the course are available, and publicize the TA locations and office hours. Let them know if the department or college provides tutoring to help students with any of their courses. If first year students take a freshmen experience class, check with that instructor to see what they are told about these resources and also are given some time management basics, and strategies to prepare for and go to office hours. If a student continues to show poor academic performance, stops coming to class, or just seems to be struggling in general, you should contact Student Services. They can often intervene as a neutral party to help students' problem solve a course of action to avoid failure.

It is also important to take some time in your class teaching students how to study your discipline. How should they read a science or engineering textbook? How should they prepare for quizzes and exams? When they are in the testing situation, how should they approach the test? Should they take each question in order, or answer the ones they feel most confident about first, leaving more time for the questions that they find more challenging? Should they hand in their work with the quiz, so they can get partial credit, or do you just want the answers? Providing this information - especially to freshmen - is time well spent.

Try to remember that the first year student is one who is essentially still in high school mode. Whether we like it or not, many of these students will have a lower level of maturity, less refined study skills, and less preparation than we're used to in upper class courses where students are more mature, and have all met a certain prerequisite. By understanding this, and knowing how to help first year students when they struggle, we can be proactive players in their success.

Jonas

Quick Tip: Try a classroom assessment technique the first day of class. Prepare a short form of the basic knowledge that students should have coming into your class. Then ask students to anonymously check off: a) think I know it b) think I've heard about it c) you got to be kidding. The student will then have some idea of what background work they need to do and when collected, the instructor will have a whole class view of areas that might be problematic.

TEACHING PROBLEM SOLVING

Dear **Jonas**,

I'm frustrated with my students' apparent inability to tackle basic problems in my course. Their approach to these problems appears to be haphazard and usually consists of writing a bunch of equations they think will help, and then choosing the equation that appears to have the right variable names, hoping that one of the equations will be solvable. Isn't

---

there any way I can get them to solve problems in a systematic way?

Soul-searching Solver

Dear **Solver,**

Problem solving is about the integration of two complementary skills: understanding a concept or principle and applying that concept to particular sets of circumstances. Generally learning takes place in increments with understanding enhanced by application and application enhanced by deeper understanding. Learning often does require some trial and error that leads to discovery.

In math, science and engineering, we generally present or derive a concept linearly and logically. We then illustrate that principle by applying it to a particular situation. It is relatively easy for a student to observe this process step by step and agree with the process without understanding fully why the steps were taken. We're all familiar with a student saying, "I understand everything you did in class, but I don't know how to even start the homework".

We must constantly remind ourselves that we (instructors) understand the concepts fully and we intuitively know what solution strategy is best for the particular application we are presenting - but our students generally don't. It's a new experience for them. I could take a map of the Eastern US and highlight a route from Boston to New York that would work well and could be followed by someone with only the most rudimentary understanding of maps (e.g., roads are lines and have route numbers). If, however, I then asked him to highlight an efficient route from Hartford to Albany, he would probably suggest a continuous route but might include travel on secondary roads (that seem to be more direct) rather than highways.

Had I, in the first instance, not just showed the route, but explained why I made certain decisions (e.g., highways are bolded while secondary roads are not) along the way, he would have been prepared to design routes, not just follow one. I could have improved his capabilities more quickly if I had illustrated and explained my selection strategy as I sketched the route from Boston to New York or engaged him as he traced the route from Hartford asking why he was making certain decisions ("Why include that link?" "Oh yeah, I forgot that the dotted line represents a dirt road."). Intelligent trial and error is fundamental to learning and understanding. Our own efforts in research remind us of that.

Clearly, the first step in problem solving is to present the basic vocabulary and concepts. Then we move on to applications. Here we must remember to explain the "why" as well as the "how." The primary method for "teaching" problem solving is modeling your thought process as you solve problems (i.e., showing students that there is a strategy for problem solving that is not random or based on luck).

Here are some suggested general strategies for teaching a logical problem-solving method:

1. Present the problem, and be sure that it is understood (e.g., the task is to identify the fastest driving route from Boston to New York).

2. Actively engage students in identifying graphical representations, tools, concepts and strategy (at least the first step or two) that would be potentially helpful in solving the problem. Often a suggestion will be put forth that you know will not work. It is sometimes a worthwhile learning experience to pursue the suggestion until it's clear to all that it won't work and why. This should improve understanding of the concept and lead to the selection of a more informed solution strategy. It will further illustrate the interconnected nature or problem-

solving and understanding - not just the "hows" but the "whys."

3. Identify common pitfalls in solving certain types of problems (e.g., going back to our driving directions analogy, you could point out that exit numbers often change when one crosses state lines, and that this can be confusing; or, point out that people often miss the split in the road when I-95 and I-93 fork).

4. After arriving at the correct solution, you might ask your students how the problem could have been changed to make the outcome different or require the use of a different approach to solve it. You might pursue a permutation of the problem to illustrate the altered solution strategy.

5. Homework involving multiple permutations will give students practice in applying the general concept to differing situations.

You have to use your judgment on how explicit to be in this step-wise approach, but be careful about assuming that your students recognize how you got from one step to the next. Showing students that there is a logical strategy for effective problem solving will reinforce the procedural aspect of the process, and make it less like an exercise in voodoo or something one needs years of experience to master.

Students don't typically realize that we are trying to teach them general problem solving skills. They naturally expect to learn something about the subject of the course ("calculus", "physics", "chemistry", "engineering"), but they might not see the bigger picture. A clear statement in the course syllabus that one of the goals of the course is to learn problem-solving skills would be helpful. You can also provide homework or quizzes and tell them in advance that the grading will be based entirely on how systematically they approach the problems. Whether we're teaching engineers, scientists or mathematicians, technical problem-solving skills are perhaps the most valuable tool we can impart to our students. Good luck.

Jonas

> **Quick Tip:** In our research efforts, understanding is a result of our discoveries; it's the same for the students in our classes.

AN APPEAL FROM A FRESHMAN

Dear **Readers**,

As an introduction to the differences between teaching freshmen and teaching upper-classmen, I want to relate the story of a freshman engineer who entered college in the Fall of 2000. I will refer to this student as John Doe.

John Doe looked very promising on paper; his SATs were a 640 in Math and a 640 in Verbal. His high school GPA was a 3.0. However, after the Spring 2001 Quarter, John was removed from the university because of poor academic performance - his QPA was a 1.5. After the summer, John decided that he wished to return to school for the Fall Quarter of 2001, and so he wrote a letter to the Academic Standing Committee, explaining why he had performed so poorly during his freshman year, and why his performance would be different if he was readmitted.

With John's permission, I have reproduced his letter below. It is an amazing letter, which illuminates what some freshmen go through in making the transition from high school to college. John Doe's letter was successful: he was readmitted, on probation. I hope that you will read John's letter.

Jonas

John Doe's Letter to the Academic Standing Committee

I remember my first day at school – the excitement I felt as I packed the night before, the good-byes to friends and family, and the actual drive down. My parents helped me get settled before they too wished me luck and said their farewells. After the door closed and I was at last on my own, I remember lying down on the bare mattress and looking up at the ceiling, deep in thought. This is it; I'm finally here. After 18 years of living under someone's else's rule I was finally free...free go where I wanted, free to come home when I pleased, and free to party until my legs would no longer support my body weight. This was it; college, where everyone has the time of their lives.

In all honesty, this was my reality. I was now in the stage of leaving home and attending college. I had a very naïve perspective from early on in my life, coming from a small town in Iowa where everyone at school had known each other all of their lives and the rest of the world didn't seem to exist. According to my teachers, I was intelligent, and my parents had always expected me to eventually go to college. This was so drilled into me that by the time I actually graduated from high school I didn't stop and think about why I would be leaving to spend four years at college, other than the idea of my experiencing freedom.

Unfortunately, my roommates had a similar outlook on the freshman experience. The only one who fully grasped why he was there didn't get along with the rest of us and eventually isolated himself completely from our group. When the other four were together we were four times worse than your average irresponsible student who was on his own. We would joke about how we hadn't studied for tests; brag about how many classes we skipped, and tease each other if one of us actually sat down in an attempt to do some homework. We weren't a group of students working to get degrees in order to be successful; we were kids who had justified treating our lives as if they were in one big game. We felt we were the rulers of our world and had the times of our lives; but in the end every one of us found ourselves scrambling to hit the rewind button while hoping it wasn't too late.

Two of us were able to somehow scrape by, but the other two were much too far behind to even come close. Every one of us, however, had to face the reality of getting up in the morning and seeing a possible failure looking back at them in the bathroom mirror. I was the third out of four friends to fail my classes.

After my depression from failing subsided, I decided that it was time for me to change. My cousin in Los Angeles offered me a room in her apartment, provided I pay rent and do my fair share of chores. My new mission then became to experience the real world and hopefully find a path in life. As my cousin so frequently pointed out, I had to learn how to be the manager of my own life, which meant deciding what my future would be.

After only a month of working in the city and supporting myself I became more optimistic about my options. I finally felt in control of my own life.

It had taken me a long time to find a decent job. Armed with my resume and two new suits from a local thrift store, I traveled from corporation to corporation in search of position where I could work with computers, my one passion. With no degree and stiff competition due to high unemployment rates, I ended up settling for a temporary position working for a company selling home products. This was exactly the type of work I had reluctantly done for four years in our family business back in Iowa, where I worked for my father publishing calendars.

But with no other options and my cousin breathing down my back about rent, I had no choice but to work a job I hated for the money. Nonetheless, my life was looking up. I was more responsible than I had ever been before, and my depression was completely gone. Eventually, I realized that having responsibilities required self-discipline and hard work but also resulted in a sense of accomplishing goals and building a future. The only thing missing from my daily routine was having a job that I enjoyed getting up for in the morning.

I had originally planned to stay in the city for a full year to re-group and find some direction. After only two months, however, the full scope of what I had given up at college and the opportunity I had taken for granted was completely apparent to me. I regret not taking time off right after high school to experience the things in life that have given me this new perspective. I could have saved myself time and money as well as avoided the overwhelming feelings of sadness and failure. As I think back and remember everyone I came in contact with at college, I realize that there were a lot of students going through exactly what I was; lost with a feeling of traveling down a path that had been chosen for them and not by them.

When I think about the roommate who we never got along with, who criticized us much of the time for our priorities and always getting straight A's, it is now with a new sense of respect that comes only with increased understanding. I understand now that if I become overwhelmed by the workload I should seek assistance. I know the snowball effect of procrastinating leads to impossible amounts of work and ultimately probable failure. I have learned that I am the only one who can determine my future. It's up to me to make better decisions about achieving my goals. But most important of all I learned that going to college is something I am fortunate to be able to do and I'll not waste the opportunity a second time. I feel that given the chance to come back and prove myself to the university I will show everyone the changes I have truly undergone.

Quick Tip: Don't hesitate. If a freshman student seems to be floundering, chances are he/she is floundering. Be proactive and arrange to see them individually as soon as possible.

FRESHMEN SWITCHERS

Dear **Jonas**:

As I was leaving class today I overheard two of my freshmen engineering students talking about transferring to another major. They are both doing fine academically in my course, but seem to be overly discouraged. I think they'd be great engineers, and I'm not sure why they want to change or what I can do about it?

Puzzled Professor

Dear **Puzzled,**

Students don't change majors just because of the degree of difficulty or rigor of a single course or a subject. There are number of reasons why students decide to do something different.

Actually, Seymour and Hewitt (1991) did a study of good students (650 Math SAT and above) who stayed in engineering as well as those who switched, and found some interesting reasons that good students change majors. They reported that some students simply lost their initial interest in science as they broadened their exposure to other areas and occupations. Many students, whether they switched or not, also felt that non-SMET (Science, Math, Engineering & Technology) majors were more interesting or offered a better education. Another reason was cited regarding the academic load: even good students felt overwhelmed by the pace and academic load of the engineering curriculum. There just seemed to be too much to do in too little time while their non-engineering roommates were going for pizza with the gang.

The last reason cited the culture of SMET. Students in this study perceived the curve-grading system widely used by SMET faculty as reflecting disdain for the worth or potential of most underclassmen. They presumed that this grading system was a way to drive a large number of freshmen out of the major, and that the curve-grading system did not provide useful feedback on their understanding of the material. They also viewed the harsh competitive grading system as discouraging the collaborative work that they knew from past experience worked well for them.

SMET faculty were perceived by these students as "unapproachable or unavailable" to help them with either academic or career planning concerns. Students saw their SMET faculty and graduate TA's as too busy with research, grant writing, conferences, and professional responsibilities to really take time to teach well. Whether this is true or not, over 93% of students who changed majors, and even 86% of those who persisted, listed poor SMET teaching as a concern.

What can YOU do? If you are working hard at your teaching and making yourself available to your students, then maybe just talking to them about your love of your subject area and why you went into it would be useful. You can also look at your own time management. Do you find that your days are so filled that you don't have much time to see your students? While we are all busy, finding ways to connect with students (e.g., sending e-mails or putting your course on the

Blackboard web site with a discussion board that you access from anywhere sends students the message you take your teaching seriously. Try having mid-course feedback mechanisms for students so you can gauge the pulse of the class. You don't have to simplify or waterdown your course, but you should think about how to help good students (who are overwhelmed and possibly overloaded) manage their workload.

Please remember that yours is not their only class; while things may be going well for students in your class, they may not be going well in others. Try connecting with other faculty who teach your freshmen and see just how much work everyone is assigning and if you are making enough connections between the courses for students to see the relevance of all they're doing. Lastly, sometimes the best thing to do is help the student make a smooth transition to another major where they'll be happy!

Regards, **Jonas**

Quick Tip: Checkout the sources of your career or counseling center; that way you'll have the name of someone your students can talk to if they are uncertain about their choice of major.

STUDENT BACKGROUNDS

Dear **Jonas,**

I am teaching a freshman class, and have found myself befuddled. There is such a variety of background preparation levels in my class, that if I go slowly enough for the students who have never seen this material before, 1/3 of the students are sleeping. If I go fast enough for the advanced students, 1/

3 of the students are lost and complaining. However, if I'm lucky, 1/3 think the class is just at the right pace. What do I do?

Goldilocks

Dear **Goldilocks**,

This is a fact of life as well as an exciting challenge of teaching first-year students. It will take some time for them to all get to approximately the same level. One consolation is that they are accustomed to this, and may have experienced it in other classes, so that they may not be as disgruntled as they appear. But there are various strategies that may help in handling the situation.

The first step you can take is to determine the different levels of preparation in the class. You can have the students fill out a brief questionnaire describing their backgrounds and experiences in the subject area. You might also ask them about their confidence in their preparation. In some cases, a short quiz, not for credit, can help. After reviewing these, talk with some of the students who have an extensive background to see if they took the AP exam in the subject; ask them if they would be willing to help some of their classmates with the material, or explore other options for having the advanced students participate in a different way in the class. I also like to let the more knowledgeable students know that I recognize that they are at a more advanced level, and that I may call on them, or ask them to help others.

Another strategy is to discuss the situation openly with the class. Describe the situation and how it affects the pace of the class for each of them. If the students understand that there are classmates at different levels, they will often be more patient if they are ahead and work harder if they are struggling. I like to say to them, if one of you knows 8 things, and another knows 6 things and someone different knows 5, each of you may pick up a limited number of new things, but my goal is to have you all learn and know about the same 10 things. You can look for suggestions from the class at this point for handling the challenge, but be careful of creating individualized courses for each student. Remind the class also that they can achieve a deeper understanding of the material by seeing it again in this class, presented in a different way.

If you have a small number of students who are at an advanced level, you may be able to give them special projects to work on outside of class to show their skill, and attend a limited amount of classes. You may want to require them to take tests or quizzes, and attend particular classes on specific sections of material. Generally, they would need to take the final exam. This requires some time for you outside of class, but can be very rewarding. An excellent suggestion that I received was to have students help write problems to use in the class or for homework, where they also must develop the solutions.

You can also use the more advanced students to assist the struggling students. You can require them to assist in class, or in labs, or help a particular student. If you are doing any group-work in class, you can place a skilled student with a group of less-skilled students, and ask him or her to be proactive in helping the rest of the group to learn.

I have been addressing the problem of having blocks of students who have had various levels of preparation. Another common problem is that of having just one or two students who seem to be significantly less prepared than the others – students who ask many, many very basic questions. These students can significantly slow down an entire class. My strategy for dealing with these students is very different from what I described above. If the less prepared students ask a question about a topic which I sense that everyone else understands thoroughly, I will try to answer the question quickly, and end my answer with "Think about it, and then, if you still have the question, ask me again after class or stop by my office during conference hours." There is a fine line that one has to walk here: One does not want to make the less prepared student feel badly, but, on the other hand, one must maintain an appropriate pace for the rest of the class. You might also speak to the less prepared students outside of class, and suggest that they come to your office hours more often.

These are some strategies for meeting the challenge. Getting it just right is difficult, but some combination of these suggestions may help with the struggle.

Jonas

Quick Tip: Have students who know the material come to the board or to the computer (in a computer classroom) and demonstrate a technique or solve a problem; it keeps them involved. Often they understand the common trouble areas, because they have just experienced them. Ask them to discuss their initial errors as others will have made them as well.

ROLE MODELS

Dear **Jonas**,

I just attended a teaching seminar here at Northeastern University that focused on first-year students, and the speaker mentioned that faculty should be conscious of being a role model as we go about our business. To be honest, I feel a bit like Charles Barkley, the professional basketball player and author of "I May Be Wrong But I Doubt It," who announced that he didn't want to be a role model; I don't either. I've got enough to do with teaching, scholarship and service. When did being a role model become part of this job?

Recalcitrant Role Model

Dear **Recal**,

The good news is that you don't have to make this decision about being a role model. The bad news is that you already are, whether you like it or not. You can't avoid this; it
comes with the territory. In fact, we lose a lot of students
because of the role models that students see in their instructors and graduate students. As a faculty member, we interact
with students in class, in our offices, and when we see them
around campus. Believe me, they are watching to see not only
what we know, but what we do, how we behave, and who we
are!

But what does this idea of being a role model really
mean? Some students may see faculty as "nerds" or "geeks".
But it's much more than that. In our own lives we look for
role models who are passionate about what they do and show
it, who are respectful and care about us and our work; who
are genuine and who personify the principles they espouse.
For a teacher, then, this means many things. First of all, there
is the issue of respecting students, which we can show in so
many ways: being on time and prepared for class, not putting
them down when they ask questions (even if we've heard a
particular question a hundred times), and making sure we're
there for our scheduled office hours. When we don't do these
things, we're sending a message to the student (sometimes
subtle, sometimes not) that they're not important enough for
us to make this effort. Whether we like it or not, our personal
appearance also says something about both our respect for
the students and our professionalism. If you come to class
looking like you just finished exercising and forgot to shower,
then you are sending the message to students: "I don't care
enough about you or respect you enough to at least look pre-
sentable before coming into this classroom." Similarly, you
should not be using obscenities or other inappropriate language during lectures or in one-on-one conversations. Most

students will perceive it as disrespectful, unprofessional, and/ or a cheap way to somehow connect with them.

This idea of respect is also connected to our being concerned about our students' success. We should want our students to succeed, and do what we can to help them get there. Let's be clear: this doesn't mean that we coddle them or inflate grades. It means that we give frequent, timely feedback in class and on assignments that will help them to do better the next time around. It means correcting and guiding them (again, in a respectful way) when they are doing something wrong, academically or even with their behavior in class. As an undergraduate, I vividly remember failing Professor K.'s first exam and feeling devastated. In a conversation with me after class, he said he understood that I must be disappointed. He let me know this can happen to anyone and reminded me that his grading system would eliminate this poor grade if we did better the rest of the way. Fundamentally, he convinced me that he cared about my success; I remember feeling that I did not want to let him down. Ultimately, I earned an "A" in the course.

Faculty who "go the extra mile" for students will be remembered long after those students have taken your class. This "extra mile" can be anything from staying a little later than normal to give some extra help, to being compassionate when they're having some personal problems. We should also be willing to collect feedback from them on our performance as teachers, listen and then respond thoughtfully to what they say.

Your enthusiasm for your subject area is also important. You went into this field because it fascinated or intrigued you; remember to tell students that. You have stories from your research and practice in your field that students want to hear. By the way, these "war stories" also help to spice up your lectures and show your passion for what you do and reveal a little about who you are and what matters to you. When you are presented with a student's question, do you see it as an opportunity to teach something about the subject? Or do you sigh and wish you hadn't left your office door open? Again, students see these verbal and non-verbal cues and draw conclusions about you, and about your interest in them as students, the subject matter, and your job. If they're receiving negative messages from you, it's only natural that they wouldn't want to become a nurse, chemist, or engineer.

Your professionalism is a major component of role modeling. Being respectful when you talk about other's work that you may not agree with, acknowledging there may be other views on an issue, refusing to enter into public griping: these all show students that while you may disagree, you respect your field and those who have worked hard in it.

Most importantly, role modeling involves letting students see you as a person, being genuine, and not some image of a professor. Don't be hesitant to discuss the things that matter to you: a hobby, traveling you've done, your family, etc. Even when students hear about a conference I've been to, they are often interested (and frankly, amazed) that people get together and talk about a particular research area, or that those opportunities exist. These are the kinds of things that help you, as a faculty member, connect with students, and they start to see you in a different way: as the person you are. Students can spot a phony a mile away, so let them see the real you. They may learn more from that than some of the course material you're trying to teach them.

Being a role model shouldn't be hard work, but it does require an awareness on your part that students are constantly checking out how you do things, how you interact with them, and how much of what you say matches what you do. And whether we like it or not, it's part of our job, whether we're teaching students, supervising research, or advising a student group.

Good luck, **Jonas**

Quick Tip: Before making a decision involving a class or an individual student, it is often helpful to ask ourselves: what would I do for my son or daughter in that same situation at the same stage in his/her development? This doesn't mean that we always give the student or class a break. Sometimes the more difficult choice is the best answer, but at least we are making the judgment in the best interests of the student's development.

Chapter 4

Dear Jonas:

Don't They Teach Them Anything in High School Anymore?

Susan Freeman

Picture this: you just got your teaching schedule, and on it this year is an entry-level course in Calculus, or Programming or English. Undergraduate students? Is that like teaching High School students? Well, not exactly, but college life may still be fairly new, so the class is going to have some challenges that do not exist in your upper level or graduate level course. Even with many years of teaching experience, you may find that some retooling of your teaching techniques is needed, and that is the focus of these Dear Jonas columns. The columns in this chapter discuss classroom activities and teaching strategies and approaches that may be applicable in any classroom, but are particularly effective to the teaching of undergraduate students. Specific classroom issues, such as communications, teacher/student interaction, and student development are addressed in later chapters.

Here's an example of two real scenarios of the best and worst first day of class. It is the first class of the fall term, and there are about 25 students in the room, a manageable number. They walk in and seem eager to be there, responding warmly to hello. I introduce myself, tell them what the class is about in general terms, and then spend a little time telling them about myself. I hand out the syllabus; they pair up and come up with some good questions about the course. I have them make name placards, and take Polaroid pictures of them to learn their names while they fill out information sheets. We even have time for everyone to introduce himself or herself and tell the class one interesting thing that happened in the summer. Everyone seems pleased and comfortable from the start.

Then there is my worst first class scenario. It is a slightly larger class, and there are not enough seats for everyone. Due to the grumbling, which I ignore, there is little response to my greeting. I hand out the syllabus, which they immediately tuck away. I start right in on the material, only to find out that they have not purchased books. As I begin the class, they appear not to be engaged with my lecture as some students are chatting and others are reading. At the end of class, the students leave feeling somewhat disgruntled, and I feel like I have not accomplished anything.

The differences between the two days are not the class size or room, though we often blame these factors. In the best day, my emphasis was on forming relationships, setting expectations for the course, and taking cues from my students. In my worst day scenario, I was concerned with getting the material to them and getting started. I quickly learned to have a first class much like the one Jonas describes in his first column. Students have told us that they want to know who we are, that we care and are approachable, that we are excited and interested to be teaching them, and that we will get to know each of them individually.

In this chapter, starting with the first class of the term, Jonas gives some discussion on the importance of forming relationships, and setting expectations for the class. Once into the course, the concept of time management for each class, and the entire course becomes important, there is so much material, so little time. Moving into the class itself, Jonas spends time on deciding what we need to teach, and how to choose the course material. Now that we are in the throes of the term, Jonas identifies some non-facilitating teaching behaviors that we all recognize are easy to slide into. Motivting freshmen to see the importance of homework to their learning is next. While in the midst of all of this, we need to get some feedback from our colleagues and students, so Jonas discusses some ways to do that effectively. Lastly, Jonas then describes one mode of facilitating cooperative learning in the class, through "paired programming." One way of doing that is through Peer Review, or what Jonas renamed GET FIT - Faculty Interactions about Teaching. This type of review is not an evaluation of teaching, but an opportunity for faculty to get together and talk constructively on how the teaching is going and how it can be improved. Jonas invites faculty to try it.

The amount of literature on teaching, and teaching first-year students is considerable. One of the most popular and most recommended is W. McKeachie's (1999) *Teaching Tips*. This book includes tips and strategies, but also the research and theory that form the foundation for these strategies. Lowman (1995) effectively organizes a lot of material on teaching and learning in a way that helps teacher adapt existing strategies, and adopt new strategies to improve student learning in the classroom. In Orlich et. al. (1994) there is material on planning your course and making teaching decisions, but there are also sections on questions and discussions, and getting our students to use higher thinking skills. In Champagne (1995), there is similar material as the other texts, but this book is organized around questions to challenge the reader, and discusses teaching versus learning. Gullette's work (1984) contains a collection of writings from the Harvard-Danforth Center for Teaching and Learning, covering most aspects of teaching in the University. Erickson and Strommer (1991) have focused on teaching freshmen. They start with understanding freshmen, then teaching freshmen, followed by special challenges for teaching freshmen. This text still covers teaching strategies, yet focuses on the differences and the importance of the differences between freshmen and upper classmen. It still addresses most of the traditional topics, such as learning styles, setting goals in the classroom, active learning, evaluating the classroom, and grading.

Teaching skills, good teaching strategies, assessing what the students are learning, assessing our teaching - these are subjects that concern any University faculty. But in teaching undergraduates we need to be especially sensitive and tuned into our students, into how they are doing and what they are learning. This chapter focuses on classroom activities and teaching tips for keeping our students connected and "setting them up for success"!

Further Reading

Books

1. Champagne, David W. (1995). *The Intelligent Professor's Guide to Teaching.* Weston, FL: ROC EdTech.

2. Erickson, B. L., Strommer, D. W.(1991). *Teaching College Freshmen.* San Francisco, CA: Jossey-Bass Publishers.

3. Gulette, M.M. (Ed.) (1984). *The Art and Craft of Teaching.* Cambridge, MA: Harvard University Press.

4. Lowman, J. (1995). *Mastering the Techniques of Teaching.* San Francisco, CA: Jossey-Bass Publishers.

5. McKeachie, W. J. (1999*). Teaching Tips: Strategies, re-*

search, and theory for college and university teachers (10th ed.). Boston, MA: Houghton Mifflin.

6. Orlich, D. C., Harder, R. J, Callahan, R. C., Kauchak, D. P., Gibson, H. W. (1994). *Teaching Strategies, A Guide to Better Instruction.* Lexington, MA: D. C. Heath and Company.

Articles

1. Atman, C. J., and Nair, I. (October 1996). *Engineering in context: An empirical study of freshmen students' conceptual frameworks.* Journal of Engineering Education, 85 (4): 317-326.

2. Besterfield-Sacre, M., Atman, C. J., and Shuman, L. J. (1997*). Characteristics of freshman engineering students: models for determining student attrition in engineering.* Journal of Engineering Education, 86(2): 139-149.

3. Felder, R. M. (1997*). Who needs these headaches? Reflections on teaching first-year engineering students.* Success 101, fall 1997, p. 2.

4. Felder, R. M., Felder, G. N. Ditz, E. J. (1988). *A longitudinal study of engineering student performance and retention v. comparison with traditionally-taught students.* Journal of Engineering Education, 87(4), 469-480.

5. Napell, Sondra M. (1976). *Six Common Non-facilitating Teaching Behaviors.* Contemporary Education, 47(2): 79-82.

Websites

1. ASEE (American Society for Engineering Education) http://www.asee.org

2. Deliberations on Teaching and Learning in Higher Education. http://www.lgu.ac.uk/deliberations/

3. University of North Carolina Center for Teaching and Learning. http://www.unc.edu/depts/ctl/fyc.html

4. Resources in Engineering and Science Education (Rich Felder) http://www2.ncsu.edu/effective_teaching/

THE FIRST CLASS OF THE TERM

Dear **Jonas**,

As another term is beginning I'm suffering the usual anticipation anxiety. I will be teaching a section of freshman engineering students (although my anxiety is not confined to teaching freshman classes) none of whom I have known previously and none of who know me, except by hearsay from other students. While typically everything works out fine after I gain the students' trust and the class becomes responsive and interactive after a couple of weeks, the start is usually tentative and a bit uncomfortable. Any suggestions on how to accelerate the process?

Anxious

Dear **Anxious**,

I also suffer from the anxiety of anticipation with every new class of students, but that's not a bad thing. I expect that because you are thinking about getting a positive momentum going, you're probably going to achieve it as you always do. The question is, "How can an instructor speed up the development of that relationship with the new class?" The key here is to understand that while we begin any term by interacting with students, they will invest more effort and have greater expectations for themselves as these interactions mature into a mutually respectful and trusting relationship. That's just human behavior. This respect and trust, however, must be earned by your actions (and theirs); it is not simply a result of credentials or titles.

So, how do we speed up the development of this relationship? A few years ago my wife, Dusty, and I signed up for the AFS (American Field Service) program and decided to host a young woman from Denmark as she did her senior year at our local high school. Even though we had received a copy of her application materials for the program, as we were about to meet this young woman who would live with us for a year, we were excited but also anxious. The AFS program had some very good suggestions for us. For one thing, they suggested that as soon as we got back to our house, we sit down and talk about expectations (hers and ours). What should Tanja call us? We decided it would be her choice. Tanja suggested "mom" and "dad," a bit to our surprise. Other questions and expectations were discussed. What would we pay for, and what should she? Was she responsible for doing her own laundry? Was she expected to help with the dishes after dinner and do other chores? Is it our custom to leave the bathroom door open or closed? While talking, we realized that some of both our and her notions and expectations were unanticipated, and we were all more comfortable having clarified them up front.

I believe that this open and honest discussion (actually there were a few) greatly accelerated the formation of a strong relationship that still perseveres today. This same notion is directly transferable to the beginning of a new class. I always begin by introducing myself and include some personal, but not private, information. Students are often surprised to learn that a faculty member actually has a life outside of his subject material. I also ask my students to turn in a copy of their resumes at the next class, adding something personal but not private. Most undergraduate freshman students will have resumes by now. Instead of collecting resumes, some faculty create a "Student Information Form" and ask about completion of prerequisites, best way to contact students, email addresses, why they chose to take this course, etc.

Then we discuss my expectations, both of them and of myself and most importantly WHY I have these expectations for this class. Many are listed on the syllabus but not all. For example, students can ask and are encouraged to ask questions at any time. I expect a hand to be raised, but it's OK to say something to get my attention if I don't see it. I encourage students to work in groups on homework (and what that means), but each has to submit a separate solution. Late homework will not be accepted as I will distribute copies of my solutions (or put them on a website) on the due date. I explain my grading policy (grade on the final exam will be the grade for the course if better than the previous record) and why I have designed it that way. I let my students know that it's OK to be wrong in trying to answer a question in class and that I have not had a student yet who has gotten all the answers. I make it clear that I will always try to be on time for class, and if not I apologize. I expect them to do the same. I promise them that I will always be prepared for class and I expect the same from them. I expect them to review the assigned reading material (but not necessarily understand) prior to class because they will at least be familiar with terms, symbols and what I am trying to accomplish that day. I warn them that they will quickly learn that I enjoy kidding around and that some good-natured repartee is welcomed - nothing too personal though. I want them to understand that while I must set the standards of success in my course, I'll be there to help if they do their parts. If a student is not sure where she stands at any point in my course, it's OK to ask. If a student misses a class, it is her/his responsibility to get the notes from a classmate (arrange in advance if possible), go over them and then come to me with questions. I also ask about their expectations, and we discuss them.

You are obviously someone who does form a good relationship with your students. I hope my suggestions help you do this a little more quickly.

Jonas

Quick Tip: Try collecting student resumes or information forms at the beginning of a course and mention appropriate information at appropriate

---

times. If a student worked as a rigger, equilibrium concepts in a physics course would apply. When a student visits your office mentioning that he comes from Naugatuck, CT (or wherever) or that he ran the Boston Marathon, it does a lot to break the ice.

TIME MANAGEMENT

Dear **Jonas,**

I keep hearing that, to be effective in the classroom, I should begin each class by reviewing the previous class, asking if there are questions on the old material, and going over homework. Then, I should list my course objectives for the day, lecture on new material, do examples, ask the students lots of questions, let the students work on problems in class, use multimedia/technology, and perhaps throw in practical demonstrations or experiments. Oh, and I'm supposed to be sure to end each class on time.

So, I really only have one question: how the heck am I supposed to do all of those things in each class and make it through the course material?

Pressed for Time

Dear **Pressed,**

I understand your frustration. The quick answer is that one shouldn't try to force all of those things into every class, every day. Every subject differs somewhat in the arrangement (for instance, some courses have TA's who go over homework problems in detail.). I can tell you what works for me. I begin each class by going over homework for 15 minutes, focusing mainly on the most common concerns and misunderstandings. (For more advanced problems and less common errors, I post solutions on the Web or use handouts, and ask students to approach me individually with their questions.) I either preface the homework by reminding them of the basic concepts, or I remind them of the concepts in the process of going over each problem.

I then take less than five minutes to describe what new material we are going to cover that day, and indicate why we are doing it, and how it relates (or doesn't) to material that we have already covered. Then, I start on new material, and while lecturing, I try to find places where I can stop and ask the class for short answers to questions to test their grasp of the material and let them immediately apply new concepts or techniques. I do try to include a fair number of examples in my lecture and, after giving examples, I usually have the students work on short, 3-5 minute, problems. Occasionally, I have the students work on longer 10 -15 minute problems.

As for multimedia presentations, technology in the classroom, group-work, demonstrations, experiments, and other "teaching innovations", I personally use them sparingly. If a specific topic is best illuminated by one of these techniques, I will certainly use it, but I agree with you that there is not enough time to use all of these very often. What I do believe is important, and the research agrees, is that one should make his/her class interactive in SOME way every day. Maybe in experiments, demonstrations, or group work in your class would be more useful on a daily basis than having the students work individually on problems. It depends on the materials, and it does take both forethought and adjustments on-the-fly in order to fit in effective class participation. However, I'm sure that you'll find it's worth the effort.

Jonas

Quick Tip: When you ask the class a question or to work on a problem, tell the students that they have some specific amount of time to think about

---

it, say 3 minutes. Then look at your watch and make sure that you wait the allotted amount of time, without interruption. This makes certain that you actually give the students a reasonable amount of time, and also guarantees that you won't waste any class time.

TEACHING DECISIONS

Dear **Jonas:**

Is it better to teach what the students want to learn, or what we faculty feel is important to teach? My faculty colleagues (some of whom have won teaching and/or research awards) and I are struggling with deciding whether we teach class material as stated in the published departmental course descriptions, at the level we feel is necessary for subject mastery, or at a lower level, with less challenging homework assignments and tests. While we understand that we have a responsibility of educating our students at a certain level of proficiency, we often find that by pushing hard and by raising expectations, the students get frustrated. Occasionally students will simply refuse to complete an entire homework assignment, because of excessive time required to finish it.

Since our teaching is evaluated entirely by students, and our job performance is judged by our Department Head and Dean using this student evaluation, it is important that we appeal to the students' sense of quality teaching, and not alienate them. "Excessive work load" consistently contributes to a less than excellent review. In short, it is easier for a professor to do well on student evaluations by simplifying the course and making the students think they are doing just fine, then by formulating interesting and motivating, but challenging homework and tests?

The more idealistic professors will stick to their guns and do their best to teach the rigorous syllabus of course material. But it is tough to continue to be idealistic when the students criticize you for being too tough and the administration penalizes you for expecting too much of your students.

Still a Little Idealistic

Dear **Still a Little Idealistic**,

"Is it better to teach what the students want to learn or what the faculty feel is important to teach?" My answer is YES! Learning is a two way street, neither the faculty member nor the student can be held solely responsible for learning. Unless we view our students as partners in the enterprise we're doomed.

You've posed a very important question, and a short answer can only begin to address the issues. Of course faculty know what's important to teach and most definitely must have interesting and challenging assignments that stretch students and push them to their academic limits. That's what learning is all about. BUT it's not that simple.

As you pointed out there are limitations such as being evaluated only by students, though national studies and our own research here show that easy courses do not translate into higher ratings. I think motivation theory might provide a roadmap for faculty to help them retain the rigor and still meet students' needs. Research tells us that motivation or discouragement can be the result of creating disequilibria in students, BUT that positive disequilibrium is found somewhere between what's too easy (bores them and kills motivation) and what's too difficult (frustrates them and kills motivation). Careful scaffolding of supports when teaching create the right balance that challenges students and keeps them interested enough to work hard. That's important because motivation research also tells us that students will learn what they want to learn (i.e., what they are motivated to learn). So when they say, "it's too hard", they might mean "it's irrelevant" to them. Teachers should make connections between what they are presenting and why, and what the student knows, so students can perceive the value of learning the material. We know the value and relevance, they often don't.

How does one determine if positive disequilibrium has been established? Instructors have a responsibility to be fair in terms of judging the level of difficulty and the workload. If an instructor simply plows ahead with his or her agenda without adjusting for student comments (particularly if they are spread across all ability levels), then I'd argue that the instructor is not doing a good job as a teacher. There are mechanisms, both formal and informal, that instructors should use to check the decisions they've made about a course. On a formal level, most departments have an undergraduate or discipline committee where instructors can come to a consensus about course content based on student-faculty feedback. Less formal is feedback from listening to your students during the term (even inviting their comments), particularly those you believe are the best students. If strong students are struggling in a course because of the degree of difficulty or workload, the rest of the class will clearly be left in the dust. You could also use a mid-quarter evaluation that you administer to check how students are doing.

Can one be challenging and rigorous with high expectations, and still motivate students and still get good teaching evaluations? Absolutely! If you create positive disequilibrium and curiosity in students, balance support with demands, and give them some real applications, they'll work hard and evaluate you fairly. This is a simple answer to a complex question, for a more detailed explanation of how to be challenging (not overburdening) and have students work hard and learn, take a look at the book by Wankat and Oreovicz (1993) on Teaching Engineering. It's available in PDF format by chapters at www.asee.org/publications/teaching.cfm. I think it'll be worth the time and energy.

The issues you've raised are important and will be part of my columns next year: how do we evaluate teaching in a more comprehensive manner, how do we measure proficiency in the classroom, how do we motivate and not compromise, and what's the difference between pushing hard and pushing off the cliff?

Thank you for your provocative question.

Jonas

Quick Tip: Try a One-Minute Paper. Bring 3x5 cards to class and at the end of the class ask students to anonymously tell you what questions they have about the class material. You'll have instant feedback on the learning

---

NON-FACILITATING FACULTY BEHAVIORS

Dear **Jonas**,

I'm perplexed! I've been reading your column for the past year and have really come to understand the importance of engaging students in their learning. I've added a lot more discussion questions to my class, but I still seem to be doing most of the talking. Students aren't answering my questions and then I feel compelled to answer them so as to get the material across. Help! How can I get them to talk in class?

Perplexed Talker

Dear **PT**,

Ah! You've just discovered a very unsettling phenomenon. Many of us unwittingly frustrate our own teaching goals by our teaching behaviors. Often, unintentionally, we do the right thing, but in the wrong way and that only leads us to greater frustration. I, too, used to feel the same as you until I came across a wonderful article by Sondra Napell. It's from 1976 (now Jonas is dating himself), but still very valuable to think about. Napell identified what she called "Six non-facilitative teaching behaviors", in other words, behaviors teachers' employ that hinder their goal of engaging their students. Maybe you are unwittingly guilty (as I was) of some of these.

1. *Insufficient Wait Time* - Wait time refers to the amount of time between the initial question and when the teacher answers, or adds information. Students need more than just a few seconds to mentally process the information required to answer the question (Moriber, 1971, Rowe, 1974). After all, the reason you're asking a question is to get them to think. I suggest that after you ask a question, count to ten (mentally) before say anything. While this seems like an eternity in front of a silent group, they will inevitably answer if you wait.

2. *The Rapid Reward* – Accepting the first correct answer quickly favors the student who is able to rapidly process information. It also ends discussion for the more reflective students (like Jonas), who might just stop trying. Rapid reward could also create competition between rapid processors to get their hand up first. I do a couple of things to prevent myself from doing this. Sometimes I just wait again, even after a correct answer, to see who else responds and what s/he might add. I also ask students to comment on the first answer without indicating whether it is correct or not to get them to think more deeply.

3. *The Programmed Answer* - Here's an example of how typical questions of this type are phrased to the class. "Tell me, what theory you think applies to this situation? Do you think it might be the one that reflects the idea of constructing knowledge?". While this kind of guiding can be effective when you want to lead students to an answer, used on regular basis, questions of this type give the impression that there is only

one answer and the teacher knows it. It creates convergent rather than divergent thinking in your class. If your intention is to create an open exchange of ideas, try just asking the first part of the question and letting students run with it.

4. *Non-Specific Feedback Questions* - We're all guilty of this to one degree or another. How many times do we sincerely say "Are there any questions?", "Does everyone understand this?". But when you think about it, it takes a pretty confident student to admit that s/he doesn't understand what you're talking about in front of everyone else. Try being more specific about what you want to know. Ask students if they have questions about how the same principle can be applied to a slightly different situation or why you used a particular value for a variable in a problem. The more specific the question, the more likely students are to admit they're not following you, which facilitates student response to your questions.

5. *Teacher Ego-Stroking and Classroom Climate* - Have you ever said something like "the explanation should be clear now, any questions?" Again, while our intention is to help processing and understanding, our actual outcome often makes students feel that if it isn't "clear" or "obvious" there may be something wrong with them. A productive classroom environment is one where students believe that the classroom is a safe place to try out new ideas and thoughts. Eliminating judgmental phrases in questions helps, but referring to other students answers, allowing your own hesitancy or uncertainty (or ignorance) to show when answering their questions also cultivates a supportive classroom climate.

6. *Fixation at Low-Level of Questioning* - While we want our students to be critical, higher level thinkers, we often ask questions which are really information checks to test whether they 'know the facts'. Asking questions that require students to do complex thinking and waiting for an answer usually increases the level of class interaction. Instead of asking them

what formula to use, ask them why that formula is used and see what happens.

Getting students engaged in their own learning and creating critical thinkers is an important classroom goal. By looking at our own teaching a little more critically, we can often modify behaviors that get in our own way.

Jonas

> **Quick Tip:** When asking students whether they have questions, change your phrasing from "Are there any questions?" to "WHAT are your questions now?"

HOMEWORK

Dear **Jonas,**

I assigned my students some problem sets to do over the weekend. On Monday morning, I posted the solutions on Blackboard, so they could compare their answers with the correct ones. When I came into class today, I asked students if they had questions based on the homework. I got a lot of blank stares and silence. I then asked how many had done the assignment. Only five students raised their hands. I don't remember having this problem when I first started teaching. Is it me, or are students less likely to do homework than they were a decade ago?

Wondering about Work

Dear **Wondering,**

You raise a frustration felt by many faculty members. In fact, this was the topic of a recent article in the Chronicle of Higher Education (Young, J.R., "Homework? What Homework?" December 3, 2002 available at http://chronicle.com/free/v49/i15/15a03501.htm). The author and several faculty members interviewed hypothesized that students are in fact spending less time on out-of-class assignments than previous generations. Some of this may be a carry-over from the last couple of years of high school, where they may not have spent much time out of school on assignments. It may also be affected by the many commitments they have such as jobs, clubs, sports and a lack of skill in prioritizing.

There are several issues that should be considered here. We know that final course grades show a strong correlation with homework performance during the term. If you do not collect or grade these assignments, there may be a tendency on the part of students to let it slide. While you may want them to take responsibility for their learning, freshmen often lack motivation or self-discipline ("I'll do it, but not right now"). At the start of the term, emphasize that working out the problems before seeing the solutions will increase their learning, and that this practice is key to success on exams. Explain that doing homework will help them confirm what they understand, as well as identify what they need to clarify in class, tutoring meetings or review sessions.

In addition, it is important to realize that freshmen may need more structure (e.g., deadlines and feedback) than you are currently providing. The approach you mentioned probably works better with more advanced or mature students. While you may have several good reasons (such as class size) for not collecting everyone's assignments every week, it makes sense to make the students more accountable for their work. For example, you could randomly select 1-2 problems out of the homework set each week to check or grade, and let the class know that you will do this. An added bonus of this approach is that you will get feedback on what they understand and are struggling with, as well.

Once students get feedback on problems, they should be encouraged to re-work these or similar items on their own.

This activity will reinforce learning and give them practice completing the task correctly.

You might consider using a web-based homework assignment system. A few systems (e.g. http://hw.utexas.edu/) are available to go along with common introductory texts in calculus, physics, and chemistry. These systems make it possible to assign individualized problems to the students, automatically grade and record scores, and provide the students with immediate feedback about which problems they got right and wrong. You can also set up the system so that they can rework and resubmit problems they get wrong. The disadvantage to these systems is that you are generally limited to problems with numerical or multiple-choice answers, and the students are graded only on the answer and not on the method. But if a web-based homework system is combined with other components of the course that provide more feedback on methods and approaches, this combination can lead to very effective teaching in large classes.

Another concern is not only the amount of time students spend on homework, but how they spend that time. Are they being productive? For instance, do they know that research shows that students who study in groups perform better than those who study alone? For an example of this, see a report on Uri Treisman's research in freshman Calculus courses, at http://vccslitonline.cc.va.us/mrcte/treisman.htm. It is worthwhile for you to coach your class on HOW to approach the assignment, and under what conditions. (Should they time themselves? If so, how much time should they allow? Do they know what resources - such as TA office hours and online help - are available? Should they do the work open-book or closed book? With or without calculators?)

Finally, the students should know why they are being given the assignments. Let them know if they will be expected to be familiar with basic information before they can do the next assignment or in-class project, or how future concepts build on these skills. Help them see the value of the effort, and that it is not "just busy-work".

One frustration I hear frequently from students is that some professors give homework that seems unrelated to exam questions. If your goal in assigning problem sets is to prepare students for exams, make sure questions are worded in similar ways and are equally difficult. If your exam questions are application-oriented and the homework is more practice-oriented, include a few samples in their assignments of the sort of test items they are likely to encounter and make target solutions available.

It is wise to discuss your expectations on assignments and suggestions for completing them, early in the term. Some professors invite former students who successfully completed the course to give pointers to new students on ways to do well. They may reinforce the importance of doing problem sets. It's a good idea to re-emphasize these points periodically throughout the course, particularly before exams and when returning graded exams.

Jonas

Quick Tip: The next time you assign homework, alert students about which problems are particularly challenging or more complicated than they appear. Your comments will serve as an alert to help students budget their time and energy accordingly.

PEER REVIEW OF TEACHING

Dear **Jonas:**

I've been teaching the same course to first year students for many years. Once again this quarter, I'm frustrated that I don't know how students are responding to my teaching, and I won't know until I get the standard teaching evaluation back well after the quarter has ended. I did administer a mid-quarter assessment survey of my own. That provided some feedback, but just didn't probe deeply enough to allow me to make practical modifications to my teaching. I'd like to use a more comprehensive tool during next quarter and well before the course ends. Can you help?

Starved for Feedback

Dear **Starved**:

As a matter of fact, there's a new program that the Master Teaching Team has just started which can provide instructors of freshman courses with comprehensive, confidential feedback on their teaching during the quarter. It's called Get Fit – Faculty Interacting on Teaching, and it's administered for us out of the University's Center for Effective University Teaching (CEUT). The confidential results of the assessment are known only to you and your colleague reviewer, a fellow faculty member. The CEUT collects the final results of the visit, and may use aggregate results without names for research purposes. Currently, the Get Fit team consists of instructors on the G.E. Master Teaching Team. They have received training on the process and have practiced the technique by peer reviewing each other.

Here's how it works: if you want to be have a peer visit for a particular course, contact either your department representative on the G.E. Team, or the CEUT. The names and e-mail contacts are listed later. The CEUT will identify a peer colleague who is not in your department to do the visit. It's important to emphasize that this is not about the course content, but rather it focuses on teaching style. The visit is actually more effective when someone from outside your area assesses the effectiveness of your class (so s/he is not distracted by the material itself). Your peer visitor will be from the G.E. Team since those are the individuals trained to date. You and your colleague will set up a pre-meeting to talk about the class, any concerns you have, particular things you'd like them to look for, and logistics (when, where, etc.). The colleague will attend one of your classes and do the assessment based on a set of guidelines that were recommended during the training s/he received. A day or two after the class, you both will meet and go over the joint impressions of how the class went, and the peer colleague reviewer will also write a follow-up letter so that you have a hard copy of the review results. A little later on, the CEUT will ask you to provide a review of the process and its usefulness.

I want to emphasize that the report resulting from the visit is strictly meant for you, the instructor, to use for improving and/or modifying your teaching. The results are not shared with your dean, department chair, course coordinator or anyone else; you, of course, are free to utilize the letter if and as you wish. The Get Fit process is designed as a constructive one to help you figure out what you're doing right, and what changes you might make to be an even better teacher.

I encourage you to try Get Fit. I am confident that you will find it to be beneficial.

Jonas

Quick Tip: Call today and schedule a Get Fit peer visit!

PAIRED PROGRAMMING

Dear **Jonas,**

I am teaching an introductory class, and some of my students asked if they could work on their assignments together. They said that they had worked in pairs in another engineering class, and felt that it worked well, so they wondered if they could do it again. They told me that they handed in one homework assignment for two people. I have always encouraged them to form study groups and help each other, but insisted they submit individual work. Have you encountered this approach before?

Paired What?

Dear **Paired,**

The students may have been referring to a technique called "Pair Programming," which is used in some programming courses in the College Of Engineering. Pair Programming involves students working as a team of two on specifically designated aspects of the same design, algorithm, computer code, or assignment. The primary objective of using Pair Programming is to reduce students' frustration when programming for the first time and to increase the likelihood that they will continue attempts to understand the nuances of computer programming more easily than when working alone. This type of partnership may be extended to other types of assignments, but requires that the students assume very specific roles.

Pair Programming is not merely an exercise in dividing up required work on a coding project. For each assignment each member of the pair has an explicitly defined role of being either driver or navigator. The driver has control of the pencil, mouse, or keyboard and writes the code. The navigator continuously and actively monitors the work of the driver, watching for defects, thinking of alternatives, looking up resources, and considering strategic implications of the work. The team members work under these specific guidelines and are instructed to cooperate on the entire assignment together, rather than dividing it up and integrating the parts later. They are also expected to schedule time together for the purpose of completing their joint work. Partners are required to trade roles for each new assignment. All students must participate in Pair Programming for at least one assignment. Quizzes and tests are taken individually, so the students are still accountable for learning the material in the course.

Assessment done by faculty using Pair Programming found that it inspired confidence in the students, specifically in their ability to achieve the task at hand. Team members reported that they benefited from exposure to their partner's ideas and suggestions, and that they achieved a broader understanding of the requirements for assignments. Students indicated that it was easier and quicker to complete their work and expressed an overwhelming belief that it helped them identify errors more readily and consider alternative approaches to problem solving. Correlation of student grades with their reported time logs supports student accounts of their experiences. A typical comment from a student who participated in Pair Programming follows:

> Without the roles that we were working in, finishing this assignment would have been much more difficult. Instead of working with one person's ideas, we used two sets of ideas, and pooled them together in order to produce an answer to the assignment.

From an administrative perspective, Pair Programming enables more efficient use of the university's facilities and resources, since fewer workstations are required. The instructors' time is also better utilized, since the number of potential inquiries is reduced, and the quality of inquiries is improved.

Two experienced professors, who have employed Pair Programming techniques, noted that the tone of the lab environment was distinctly more collegial and less stressful than in courses where students worked individually. Students conveyed a higher perceived level of satisfaction in courses and with projects that make use of Pair Programming. Higher levels of learning are achieved, because partners can more readily solve minor problems, such as syntax errors, and move on to more complex issues. Homework grades were higher for Pair Programming participants. In addition, students reportedly gave up less often and were likely to submit more complete projects than when working alone. These benefits resulted from strict adherence to explicit roles.

Successful implementation of Pair Programming does require a level of diligent administration. To ensure that students maintain their roles, they are required to submit time logs and report percentages of work done individually on each assignment. Some students do find it difficult to meet with classmates outside of class, and therefore the instructor cannot be guaranteed that the teams are following the guidelines. Faculty work with the students to ensure adherence to the guidelines, and feedback on Pair Programming is solicited frequently to assess the implementation.

When working as Pair Programmers, students performed just as well in the course, learned as much programming and achieved good scores on tests and quizzes, but were considerably less frustrated; they related that they actually enjoyed programming. The fostering of student learning through pairing is likely to enhance student learning in other venues as well.

Jonas and Partner

> **Quick Tip:** The following linked articles provide more information about Pair Programming along with suggested methods for administering it in a class. These articles appear on the GE Master Teachers website.

Chalk Talk – E-advice from Jonas Chalk

Chapter 5

Dear Jonas: What Can I Say?

David Massey

Anyone who has taught has encountered the problem of what to say to students in order to create a learning environment where faculty and students' responsibilities are carried out in a reasonable fashion. The class responsibilities for students include: showing up for class and paying attention, documenting acceptable excuses for missing tests or due-dates, coming to the instructor's office hours if they need extra help, and communicating with instructors outside the classroom when necessary. For faculty these include: having a detailed syllabus, formulating clear guidelines for grading, and constructing clear directions for assignments; all aspects of good communication.

The scenarios that we often encounter would frequently be humorous if we saw them in a movie, instead of in our own classroom: an instructor asking questions to a class, and seeing nothing but far-away, glazed, looks on faces; far-fetched excuses on the part of students for missing classes or turning in work late; the desperate failing student who does not know what else they can do to improve their grade and, yet, has not once graced your office hours; or the students who are masters of the Internet for communicating with their friends, but then claim that they did not think of e-mailing their instructor over the weekend with a question about an assignment. The challenge for faculty is to communicate with students in a way that not only points out the area of difficulty but also gives feedback in a way that actually creates changes in student behavior.

The Jonas columns in this chapter all address the question of how one can communicate effectively with one's students. Of course, this is such a broad topic that it overlaps with other chapters of this book. Communication in teaching is as important as communication in any relationship. It is something that must worked on in order to be successful.

The first column, "Inattentive students", is on the familiar problem of students who do not pay attention in class. The column addresses difficulties that arise both in large and smaller classes, and when the course-content is very technical.

Jonas's advice on this matter makes it clear that the issue involves changes on the instructor's part that will lead to changes in the student behavior. Jonas suggests that students need to be engaged and that the class needs to be dynamic. The instructor must do more than simply lecture: demonstrations, real-world examples, group work, and enthusiasm are all important. There is an abundance of literature that supports Jonas' recommendations. Penner (1984), Chickering and Gamson (1987), Ruhl, Hughes, and Schloss (1987), and Bonwell and Eison (1991) all agree with and enlarge upon the points made in this column. In addition, the "10-2 squared" method recommended by Jonas is a version of the Interactive Lecture developed by Johnson, Johnson, and Smith (1991). Another Jonas column that addresses similar issues is the "Time management" column from Chapter 6.

The next several columns are related to student excuses. The first two, written approximately a year apart, are related to the column "Attendance" from Chapter 6, which also deals with issues related to student excuses. The student excuse columns in this chapter suggest that having a firm policy that is laid out on the syllabus is essential. However, dealing with student excuses is such an integral part of the teaching experience, that we decided it was worthwhile to write a second, longer column, "Student excuses", in which we address student development issues and students' perception of fairness. Perry (1970) points out that many students are in the duality stage of their development, and thus perceive many issues in black and white terms. Therefore, it is especially important to be careful in establishing a policy that seems fair to both the individual students and to his/her classmates. "But the dog ate my homework" addresses concerns about students who do not complete their assignments.

The two columns on office hours deal with very real issues we all face in holding office hours. The first column, "Lonely office hours", discusses how to get students to come to their instructors' office hours. The second column, "Effective use of office hours", offers practical tips to instructors on how to make the best use of their office hours after the students actually turn up. The dynamic of reviewing material in an instructor's office is significantly different than the in-class experience, and many students find the thought of attending office hours frightening. The instructor needs to repeatedly encourage and remind students to come to office hours, make the students comfortable once they do come, and should then together discuss concepts or work on problems with the instructor's guidance and undivided attention. A lengthier treatment of these tips and issues can be found in the section "Holding Office Hours" in Davis (1993). The flip side of this issue is addressed in the column on "Students Monopolizing Time". This is followed by a piece on another important aspect of faculty communication: "Team Teaching".

The last two columns in this chapter deal with the perils of modern communication problems. The first column, "Managing e-mail communication", addresses the issue of being overwhelmed with e-mail messages from students. In the final column of this chapter, we discuss means by which students can reach instructors outside of the classroom and office hours; the Internet provides a number of possibilities that did not exist ten or fifteen years ago.

The general point that Jonas is trying to make throughout all of the columns in this chapter is that, as educators, we put a great deal of effort into communicating the course material to our students; however, we also need to put substantial effort into communicating with our students about other issues in order to help our students succeed.

FURTHER READING

BOOKS

1. Bonwell, C. and Eison, J. (1991). *Active learning: Creating excitement in the classroom.* (ASHE/ERIC Higher Education Report No. 1). Washington, D.C.: The George Washington University, School of Education and Human Development.

2. Boyer, E. (1990). *Scholarship Reconsidered: Priorities of the Professoriate,* Carnegie Foundation for the Advancement of Teaching, Princeton, N.J.

3. Chickering, A. and Gamson, Z. (1987, March). S*even Principles for Good Practice in Undergraduate Education.* AAHE Bulletin, 39:7, 3-7.

4. Davis, B. (1993). *Tools for Teaching,* Jossey-Bass, San Francisco.

5. Hildebrand, M., Wilson, R., and Dienst, E. (1971). *Evaluating University Teaching,* University of California Center for Research and Development in Higher Education, Berkeley.

6. Hilsen, L. (1988). "A Helpful Handout: Establishing and Maintaining a Positive Classroom Climate," in *A Handbook for New Practitioners from the Professional and Organizational Development Network in Higher Education*, Wadsworth, E., Hilsen, L., and Shea, M. (eds.), New Forums Press, Stillwater, Okla.

7. Johnson, D., Johnson, R., and Smith, K. (1991). *Cooperative learning: Increasing college faculty instructional productivity* (ASHE-ERIC Higher Education Report No. 4). Washington, D.C.: The George Washington University, School of Education and Human Development.

8. Penner, J. (1984). *Why Many College Teachers Cannot Lecture*. Springfield, Ill.: Charles C. Thomas.

9. Perry, W. (1970) *Forms of intellectual and ethical development in the college years*, New York: Holt, Rinehart, and Winston

Articles

1. Lazerson, M., Wagener, U., and Shumanis, N. (2000). *Teaching and learning in higher education, 1980-2000*, Change May/June, 13-19.

2. Ruhl, K., Hughes, C., and Schloss, P. (1987). *Using the Pause Procedure to Enhance Lecture Recall*. Teacher Education and Special Education 10: 14-18.

Web sites

1. Motivating Students, from Tools for Teaching by Barbara Gross Davis: teaching.berkeley.edu/bgd/motivate.html

2. Large class teaching guide from the University of Maryland Center for Teaching Excellence: http://www.cte.umd.edu/

3.	"What's in a syllabus?", from the Teaching Resources Guide of the Instructional Resources Center at the University of California, Irvine: www.irc.uci.edu/trg/46.html

4.	Teaching Manual from Columbia University: www.columbia.edu/cu/tat/4_teaching.html

5.	Web Based Communications by J. Braun at the University of Georgia: www.arches.uga.edu/~jbraun/tech/comm.html

INATTENTIVE STUDENTS

Dear **Jonas**,

I teach two classes - one with 25 students, and one with 120 students. In both classes, I frequently see students not paying attention, looking bored and inattentive. Sometimes they're even asleep. I teach very technical classes, so it's difficult to have lively classroom discussions. What can I do to keep my students interested?

Professor Sandman

Dear **Sandy,**

Students find practical demonstrations and/or experiments to be very interesting. Multimedia presentations can also help break the monotony, although you might be careful about lowering the lights when students show signs of sleep deprivation. In addition, having students work on sample problems involving material that was just covered is a common, but very good, device. Even in large classes you can get students actively involved. One good technique is called "10-2 squared." After 10 minutes of lecture or demonstration, pose a question to students that applies what you've presented. Have them work with a partner for 2 minutes to formulate an answer. Then take two minutes to debrief the group.

In your smaller class, you have extra options for making the class dynamic. You can have the students work on sample problems in pairs or even in larger groups. You can follow this up by having students present their solutions to the class for discussion. In addition, the old standby of calling on inattentive students by name really does help shake them out of their daze.

In either class, it is extremely important that you, yourself, show your enthusiasm for your subject - your energy will increase theirs! Make a real effort to find points that are open for interesting discussion, even in the midst of technical subject matter; for instance, you can sometimes point out seeming paradoxes that arise from the theory, and ask the students why, in fact, these paradoxes do not occur. Also, humor injected into the class is helpful - any good speaker knows that a bit comic relief really helps to liven up a class and provides a reenergizing pause from intensity.

As a final comment, please realize that, for a variety of reasons (some having to do with heavy course demands), students frequently stay up late and get very little sleep - an individual's lack of energy and/or enthusiasm on a given day may have nothing to do with your class.

Jonas

> **Quick Tip:** When you ask a large class to work on a problem, there will always be some students who simply sit and wait for the answer. Look around, and speak to those who are not working. A humorous comment such as "ah, I see that you are doing it in your head – very impressive" or "at least pretend to be writing something" usually has the desired effect.

EXCUSED (OR NOT) ABSENCES

Dear **Jonas,**

Yesterday, one of my students came to me and said that he wanted to make-up a quiz that he missed. He claims that he had to take his roommate to the hospital. Last week, another student missed a quiz, and said that he had to go home for a family emergency. Early in the quarter, a student turned in a computer lab assignment late, saying that his disk was damaged, so that he couldn't print it out.

What am I supposed to do? Should I demand notes from

---

hospitals or parents? And, what do I do about a damaged disk? Should I let them make-up the work without even attempting to verify that they've told the truth? I don't think that students are lying all the time, but I'm sure that some of their excuses aren't true. What do you suggest?

Skeptical Instructor

Dear **Skeptical,**

I'm afraid that this is a common problem that will probably always exist. All that I can recommend is that you have a firm policy in place from the start.

In the future, make sure that your policy on making-up work is clear; putting it on the syllabus would be a good idea. I think that a reasonable policy to put on your syllabus, or to tell students on an individual basis, is that a note from a doctor or nurse is expected for medical problems, and that a note or e-mail message from an academic advisor is expected for personal issues which affect class attendance. Having an advisor approve an absence means that students don't have to tell their personal problems to individual instructors, and it also means that students can't use the same fake excuse repeatedly.

As for the disk problems, you should tell your students that such excuses are not acceptable, as computer-related excuses are just too common, and students should know that these types of problems can easily occur. They simply should not wait until the last minute to produce a printed copy of work that is to be turned in.

A firm policy on missed work is beneficial to both you and your classes; students who have taken a test, or turned in an assignment, on-time do not like it when instructors accept late work from others with little, or no, penalty. If you explain such a policy at the beginning of the quarter, no one will think that you're being unfair later.

Jonas

> **Quick Tip:** While it is essential to have a firm, clear policy on missed work, one should still be willing to allow for the fact that some circumstances are truly exceptional. Individual cases sometimes require you to exercise your discretion.

STUDENT EXCUSES

Dear **Jonas**,

I've had it up to here with student excuses for missing quizzes, exams, and assignments. Not only do they come up with the most outlandish excuses (my boa constrictor ate my ferret which ate my homework.... last month!), but they expect me to let them make up the work. They even turn in assignments from the beginning of the quarter at the end of the quarter and expect me to grade it. This is extra work for me, which I feel is not part of my job.

Why can't students just grow-up and act responsibly about their coursework?

Head About to Pop Off

Dear **Pop-off**,

I can understand your frustration with the endless excuses. When I was an undergraduate, I had a friend who had 12 grandmothers die while he was completing his undergraduate degree! Of course, many students will have valid excuses (such as illness excused by a doctor), and you are required to allow them to make up the work. Other cases are dealt with on an individual basis, and different teachers have different policies.

The best way to avoid unnecessary excuses is to make your policy very clear from the start, put it in writing, and stick to it. You should set strict deadlines for homework, with well-defined penalties for late work - then act on it. Let's face it, students are learning the rules in college, and even us "grown-ups" need deadlines (e.g., April 15). Some instructors don't accept late homework at all, while others take off a percentage or a percentage for each day late. For quizzes and/or homework, some instructors have a policy of dropping the lowest two, with no make-ups. In addition to a late homework policy, I suggest that you state a clear policy on makeup exams. I put exam dates in the syllabus, and allow students to make up an exam if they warn me ahead of time that they need to miss it because of a valid conflict, such as an athletic event. Often it's easiest to let them take it early on exam day.

However, the problem of excessive missed work and poor excuses can be exacerbated by a teacher's response to it. If you give a due date for homework and then accept some of it late without a real reason, then students will interpret your due date as a "target" or "flexible" date. When they're faced with real due dates in other courses, all except the most motivated students will let your assignments slide. This makes teaching and grading all the more difficult, and worse, some students will fall dangerously behind and may not catch up.

When students come with inappropriate excuses after missing a quiz or homework, this is an opportunity to remind them of their responsibilities as a student and that there are repercussions for their inaction. Sometimes the best learning experiences we can provide students are often the most painful for them. It also helps at the beginning of each quarter to remind students frequently of your deadlines and then taper off as the quarter progresses so each one can start developing his/her own sense of responsibility for learning.

"To make up or not make up" depends on your goal for students' growth and development. Exceptions to your guidelines are fine as long as you are clear about WHY you're allowing the exception and that it applies to ALL students in similar circumstances. Remember at this stage of development many students are in the stage Perry (1970) calls duality - that is everything is black or white so perceived fairness is an important issue. Balancing between justified student needs for extensions and the risk of fostering inappropriate student dependency is difficult. My guiding decision making principle is to do what will help students in the class become more responsible learners.

Jonas

> **Quick Tip:** If you decide to let a student make up a test, you should decide whether the student should be penalized by having to take a harder version of the test. If you decide that the student should take a test that is the same level of difficulty as the original, then you need to think about whether you need to compose a new test, or if it is fair to the rest of the class to give a make-up test that the student may have heard information about.

"BUT THE DOG ATE MY HOMEWORK..."

Dear **Jonas,**

Invariably, on the day that an assignment is due, there is a queue of students with stories of why they couldn't get their homework done on time. Naturally, this happens at the beginning of class when I am trying to get started. I have set my office and help hours according to the free time in their schedules on the days preceding homework deadlines. Clearly it is unfair to the students ready to start class to hold things up while I acknowledge each of their stories and try to make a decision on the spot and under pressure. Additionally, this "pregame show" detracts from my train of thought as I'm preparing to teach. I listen to them, but don't want them to assume because I hear them that this is permission to not hand in work that is due without a penalty being incurred. What do I do with these students without being dismissive or rude to them?

Bogged Down by the Pregame

Dear **Bogged,**

There seem to be two issues involved here. The first is students coming up at the start of class with questions, excuses and "stories", and the other being the validity of excuses for not having done the homework on time.

For the start of class problem, one approach is to outline clearly your expectations of the students in the syllabus and in class. These expectations can include their class preparation, how and when you will be collecting homework, and how and when class will start and proceed. For example, you can state that homework is expected to be turned in at the beginning of class. If it is incomplete, you could have them attach a sheet explaining what is missing, what they tried, when and if they contacted you, and what they are planning to do to complete the assignment. As they start the line-up for explanations, remind them of the procedure listed on the syllabus and proceed with class. You can restate that you are interested in their individual concerns, but that it is unfair to the rest of the class to take up class time, and you are happy to talk at other times as noted in the syllabus.

You can also mention that it is appropriate at the beginning of class, once everyone is seated, to bring up concerns or issues that affect the whole class. I start class by asking if there are questions, concerns, problems or issues concerning the homework, material covered, due dates, etc. Often, good questions can arise, but if an issue particular to an individual is raised, I ask the student to meet with me after class. It is important to be consistent in your approach: if you always

---

start class addressing questions and issues, the students will not feel the need to "bother" you before class starts, but will wait for the appropriate time. If you consistently remind them to write explanations and submit their work, and start class on time, the queuing will diminish.

The second issue is the excuses. In your expectations, you can outline how you expect homework to be done. Explain that you expect them to start the assignment early, plan for problems like computers crashing or disks not working and leave enough time for seeking help on tough portions. It is helpful for you to tell the students in advance what problems may be more difficult, and the approximate time the assignment might take. You can remind them of office and tutoring hours for seeking help. If possible, you can give interim tasks to be completed for the larger assignments, so the students do not leave the entire assignment until the last minute. Reminders of what is due are also helpful, along with reminders of expectations. Another approach is to state that you will be dropping one or two homework grades, creating an "excused" homework rather than an "excuse" homework. Everyone has a tough week once in a while, and such a policy allows for this.

Having a consistent approach outlined in your expectations, and adhering to it is not being rude, but fair. Sometimes being too "understanding" leads to inconsistency and can cause confusion for students as well as result in more problems.

Jonas

Quick Tip: On your syllabus and your expectations list, it is helpful to outline what students can expect from you, such as your being on time, returning work in a timely manner, answering questions, holding office hours and being prepared for class.

Chalk Talk – E-advice from Jonas Chalk

LONELY OFFICE HOURS

Dear **Jonas,**

I just gave their midterm exams back to my freshmen. A lot of them seem to be having trouble, but still none of them come to my office hours for help. What can I do to get my students to come to visit my office and talk with me when they're having problems, or better yet, before they have real problems?

The Lonely Professor

Dear **Lonely,**

I'm afraid that this is a common problem, especially with freshmen. Upperclassmen seem to appreciate the value of one-on-one help more. I can tell you what I do, and some things that others have found to work, but don't think that there's any one technique that will get all of your students with problems to come to you for extra help.

The first thing to do is to make sure that your students can come to your office hours, make sure that they know where your office is, and that the times of your office hours allow them to attend. Your office location should be on your syllabus and, ideally, you would have talked to your students at the beginning of the quarter about convenient times for office hours. Also, I always tell my students on the first day of class that, if my office hours aren't convenient, they should let me know, and I'll either change the times or arrange to meet individuals at other times.

After the first week or two, perhaps after the first quiz or first graded assignment, it's good to point out to your students, that you really do want them to come to your office hours. Point out that it's the best way to get extra help. Make it clear that they don't need to make an appointment - if it's your office hours, you'll be there. To try to convince my students to come to my office, I try saying to my classes, laughingly, "Please come to my office hours. I'm so lonely. I just sit there the whole time waiting for students to come by". I try to remember to repeat all of these things to my students every couple of weeks.

Two of the reasons why students don't choose to come to their instructor's office hours are because they find instructors intimidating and because they're afraid/embarrassed to let their instructors know how little they know. To alleviate that fear of being one-on-one with the instructor, I suggest to some of my students that they come to my office in groups of two or three. You may even give them a group problem or assignment that requires them to check in with you at some point. To make the students feel more comfortable with their lack of knowledge, I say to the class, with a hint of humor, "Don't be afraid of letting me know how far behind you are - believe me, I already know", or "This seems to be a difficult area for a number of you. I don't have time to go over it more in class, but I've got plenty time in office hours". This way they know they're not the only ones who don't understand.

Just to get students used to coming to their instructor's office, and to make sure that each student knows where the office is, some instructors give an assignment, for credit, that requires students to come by the instructor's office during the first weeks of classes. However, even if you do this, you should keep reminding your students, especially freshmen, throughout the quarter that your office hours are a valuable resource that you wish they'd take advantage of.

Another obstacle for students could be the location of your office. Is it situated at some remote end of campus, or tucked away in a maze of a building? Some professors hold office hours in the cafeteria or library during quieter times - it makes the process (and them) seem less intimidating, more accessible.

During those days that you expect your office hours to be extremely busy (e.g., just before or after mid-term exams), you may wish to move your office hours to a larger room, or to post a sign-up sheet on your door in 20-minute (or whatever is appropriate) increments. This avoids the student-sitting-on-the-floor-in-the-hallway syndrome, and lets them budget their time better.

Finally, never underestimate the importance of word-of-mouth. If some students do come to your office hours, it's important that they have a good experience and that they learn something and feel comfortable coming back. Word of this positive experience will get around, and encourage other students to come for help.

Jonas

Quick Tip: If you leave your office, even for two minutes, during office hours, post a BIG sign stating "Will be back" specifying when you'll return.

EFFECTIVE USE OF OFFICE HOURS

Dear **Jonas**:

Last week a student came to my office with a problem he was trying to solve on homework that was due the following day. When I asked how he would begin to address it, he simply said, "I don't know. That's why I'm here." It was clear that he wanted me to do the problem for him. I demonstrated how to solve it and articulated the steps I took at each point. Yet, I'm not sure he actually learned anything from the exercise. How could I better handle this situation in the future?

Holding Down the Home Office

Dear **Holding**:

There are several tactics you can use to evaluate students' grasp of material and support their knowledge acquisition and application of operations. Demonstrating how to solve a problem, as you did, can be a good start. You can follow up on that by giving the student a similar problem, and asking them to do it. You could also try a technique called "scaffolding" in which you are more proactive at first, giving hints or asking key questions while making sure the student is actually solving the problem. Then - after a couple of passes where you hint and support their efforts - give another problem, and have the student do it alone. In this manner, you are offering direction and support, and decreasing that support as the student gets a better handle on how to solve the problem.

Another way to begin is to simply ask the student to tell you all of the significant things s/he can see in the formula or problem. See what s/he knows, and what gaps they have in their understanding. You could also solve the problem together by breaking the problem into sections and asking the student what s/he would do at each point. Let them know if they've made a correct choice, or find out why they used that approach (to determine whether they are guessing or can articulate the law that pertains). Breaking the problem down into segments and looking at each part together can build a dialogue about the operation. It can also help you diagnose the confusion or obstacle. It can be helpful if you provide heuristics or an outline of steps that the student can follow in approaching and solving these problems.

In any case, reassure the student if s/he seems anxious, and reinforce work done correctly. Confidence is a big factor in determining learning.

It is important that you make arrangements to follow-up on the meeting. Give the student additional similar problems to do as an assignment, and schedule an appointment for them to show you what they did on their own. This reinforces new learning, and conveys the fact that you sincerely care about how they are doing. (Studies show that when students perceive that a professor cares about their learning and intellectual development, they are motivated to work harder and will be more likely to stay in a challenging class.)

Finally, it's important that you know what to do if you detect that a student's problem may go beyond comprehension and application of class material. Students are under a lot of stress, including financial difficulties, family issues, roommate concerns and pressure to choose careers. Staff at the Center for Counseling and Student Development are available to talk directly with faculty who feel their students may be troubled, depressed or showing signs of addiction. CDS staff can help you determine if a student should be referred for counseling, and how to do that in a sensitive manner.

The Disability Resource Center is another useful resource. If you are concerned that a student may have a learning disability that is impeding their ability to learn the material, feel free to contact the Center to discuss your observations.

Office hours provide a venue where significant genuine learning can take place. It's a great opportunity, so make the most of it!

Jonas

Quick Tip: If a student is struggling with the material, it may helpful to guide them on how to read and refer to the textbook (including using the table of contents and index to locate formulae and definitions), as well as provide advice on test-taking strategies.

STUDENTS MONOPOLIZING TIME

Dear **Jonas,**

I have two classes of about 35 students each. There are three students, one in the first class and two in the second, who (in my opinion) are responsible for slowing down both classes and for taking up a lot of my time outside of class. In class, I want to answers these students' questions, but they're preventing me from getting as far as I want each day with the course material. And while I want them to come to my office hours, they take up all of the allotted time and want extra time on top of that. To be honest, they're driving me crazy. What can I do?

Losin' it

Dear **Losin',**

Believe me, you're not alone in having this problem. It often seems as though 5% of our students take up 90% of our time, both with in-class questions and requests for out-of-class help. I'm glad that you want to help them, because often they are the students who really need help; perhaps they don't get it the first time, but are willing to ask questions and put in the extra hours to understand the material.

However, having said that, a first step when one encounters this type of problem is to do a bit of diagnostic work with each student. Why are they asking so many questions in the first place? You should check to make sure that they have actually taken and passed the pre-requisite(s) for your course. It's not fair to the instructor, themselves and the rest of the class if they don't belong in the class because they lack the background for it. Sometimes I give students a little "pre-test" with 5-10 questions about some fundamental information they should know for this course. I have the students grade it themselves and tell students that this is information that I count on them knowing for this course and that it will be difficult to keep up if they don't understand this material. If they do poorly, the decision is then up to the student what to do next. Some students voluntarily drop the course, others ask me where they can get the information, and others struggle but are aware that they will be struggling.

If students are asking a lot of fundamental questions, you should also speak with them about their day-to-day preparation for class. Are they doing the reading and other homework? Are they coming in late or missing classes? Make sure they understand your expectations regarding this preparation, and that it is unfair to take up class time and excessive office hours time for lax preparation on their part. If they missed class due to an emergency or illness, you should make a plan with them about working with you, a tutor or TA to catch up.

In some rare cases, you may need to refer students to the counseling center or the disability resource center to be tested for learning disabilities. This should only be done after all of your other "diagnostics" have been exhausted.

Once you've explored all of the possible causes of the problem, and come up with nothing conclusive, you'll need to find other ways to deal with these students. In class, if one of these students asks a question that I think a number of students are likely to have (or should have), I don't mind spending quite a bit of time on it. If I think that the question is of importance only to the questioner, then I try to give a brief answer. However, you really should be prepared to use some polite method of cutting off endless rudimentary questions in class. Eventually, you simply have to say something along the lines of "Well, think about it, and let's talk after class."

Outside of class is a different story. Hopefully, you have scheduled your office hours appropriately so students can attend (you can refer to Jonas columns about office hours). When students come to your office hours, help them to focus on specific areas where they are struggling by getting them to articulate their questions. Sometimes helping them to formulate the question starts them on the road to discovering the answer. You might also suggest the use of study groups with fellow students, and use of on-campus tutoring resources.

Students should recognize that you are not their "study buddy," and that there are additional, effective ways to get help with subject matter. I have found that it can be very useful to get some students to come to office hours in small groups instead of individually. When they have common misunderstandings, you can help several at once. Also, if one of the students in the group understands a troublesome concept or problem, he or she can help explain it to the others. It also forms the seeds for study groups that can provide mutual help even after they leave your office.

There will also be students who show up at office hours and simply want to talk, perhaps about issues not directly related to the course material. Don't forget your role as a mentor and role model. These students may be interested in your discipline as a possible major, or want advice about jobs, graduate school etc. If, however, these discussions stray too far afield, you should gently urge the student to refocus on the problem or issue he/she came to see you about.

Jonas

Quick Tip: When scheduling office hours, it helps to span across two or more typical class times. If a student can't make it to part of the office hours due to a class conflict, he or she can usually make it during the next part.

TEAM TEACHING

Dear **Jonas,**

I am trying to team-teach a large course with another faculty member, and I am finding it very frustrating. When I had my own course, I knew exactly what the students were seeing in each class, I could decide exactly what went on assignments and exams, and the students could come directly to me with any problems or questions. Now I seem to have to concentrate more on coordinating with my colleague than on teaching the course. Also, the students seem confused about who is responsible for the course.

The most troublesome part is that I don't know what to do when the students complain to me about the way my colleague is teaching. I'm not sure what to tell them, because in many cases I agree with their criticisms. Should I ask my colleague to change the way he is teaching? I am not comfortable with this. Much of it comes down to a matter of teaching style, and I don't feel confident enough in my notions of the best way to teach to impose these ideas on my colleague (who actually has much more teaching experience than I do). What should I do?

Team Player

Dear **Player,**

I am not surprised that you are finding special difficulties with a team teaching situation. In individual teaching, one need only worry about one's own teaching practices, while collaborative teaching requires an integration of values, philosophies and disciplines. Team teaching is not just "turn teaching". Teaching partners need to be unified and cohesive about the structure and implementation of a course. These things don't just happen by themselves; they require specific efforts and planning on the part of the collaborating teachers.

Before beginning a team-taught course, it is important

to establish a clear definition of roles. Who will set the assignments, and who will write the exams? How will the exams be graded? If any responsibilities are to be shared, you should determine who is responsible for what and how coordination will occur. A genuine collaborative effort on the syllabus often yields a more thoughtful set of learning objectives and corresponding decisions about course content. Once the course is underway, on-going communication, with meeting and planning time built in, is a necessity. Decisions should be made with a free exchange of ideas and negotiation to reach consensus. This way, all collaborators have a shared responsibility in guiding the course, and a shared accountability.

To deal with student criticisms, an atmosphere of trust and respect among the collaboration teachers must be established. This can only be done face-to-face, so meeting regularly is essential. If, for example, you have a meeting where you discuss all the feedback from students and how to respond to them, participants must feel free to mention criticisms as well as any positive feedback from students. You can set the tone by being open to constructive criticism of your teaching and encouraging your colleagues' openness to student feedback. Afterwards, you can respond to your students and explain what actions are being taken and why. It is sometimes helpful to establish a pattern of giving each other feedback through attending the first few classes, regardless of who is teaching.

But a major question remains, is collaborative teaching worth the trouble? One has to make additional efforts in team teaching in areas that don't apply to individual teaching. Sometimes, a class is so large that the work is clearly too much for one instructor, and team teaching is a practical way to divide the labor so that each instructor has a manageable workload. Beyond this sharing of labor, there are other benefits to collaborative teaching. By working closely with colleagues, one gets a chance to see and learn from others' teaching practices. A team of teachers can bring in a much wider range of expertise than a single professor. The collaboration also provides intellectual stimulation and a natural forum for discussing teaching practices as well as providing new ideas that you might experiment with in your own teaching. Collaborative teaching is much easier for (and with) some people than others. By the nature of their research discipline, some faculty will be quite accustomed to working in collaboration with peers, while others will be used to working alone. Keep this in mind when requesting or making teaching assignments.

You may be team teaching because of its benefits, or because of departmental requirements. In either situation, as in any relationship, communication between the partners is essential to success. Hope this helps!

Jonas

Quick Tip: Conduct a midterm assessment (see mid-term assessment chapter 4) and review the results together with the teaching team. This is a good starting point for a discussion on how to improve teaching practices.

MANAGING E-MAIL COMMUNICATIONS

Dear **Jonas,**

I'm feeling overwhelmed by e-mail from my students! In some quarters I teach upwards of 100 students, and shortly before a big assignment is due or an exam is scheduled, I typically receive more than 50 e-mail messages a day. I do want to provide a lot of feedback to my students – especially the first year students – but there's got to be a better way. I've told students that I might not respond immediately to e-mail sent over the weekend, yet this means I face a pile of messages on Monday morning. I've also recommended that students come to my office hours rather than mail me their questions, but alas, I usually sit alone during office hours, reading and responding to their e-mail. Any suggestions?

Relentless Replier

Dear **Relentless**:

You're not alone in feeling buried by e-mail: there are times when it can take me two hours to read and reply to a day's worth of e-mail. E-mail can bring out the closet Luddite in even the most technologically friendly professor. Yet before blaming the technology, we should analyze the type of question students are asking.

Do you find that you're writing the same reply to many different students' question? Could it be that you've not been as clear or detailed in your class assignments or lectures as you thought you were? Freshman students especially need more structure and detail than students further along in their undergraduate career. Pausing in your lecture every 15 minutes, and asking for students' questions, is a wise investment of time: better to answer a question once for all the students to hear, than to answer the same question 50 times to individual students by e-mail.

This may not offer a complete solution to your e-mail problem, however. Perhaps many of the e-mails you receive are questions related to scheduling and course policy: "Can I have an extension on the problem set?" "What day is the exam?" "When will you be returning our lab reports?" In some cases, automating your reply can be a timesaver. For example, you could compose a generic response using word processing software like Word, Simple Text or Notepad, and save it on your computer. Then copy and paste the response into your reply to students' e-mail messages. This approach is especially useful when you've taught the class before, and can anticipate the type of questions students are likely to ask.

Along similar lines, you can create a list of Frequently Asked Questions (FAQ) for your course. When students ask one of the questions on the FAQ, either copy and paste the pre-written response into your e-mail reply, or tell students to check the FAQ itself. Perhaps you could post this information outside your door or on a web site.

In many situations, however, canned responses like these will not address students' questions, and some instructors may cringe at the thought of depersonalizing their feedback in this manner. Here's where another technological tool – the online discussion board – might be a great alternative to e-mail. If you create a class bulletin board that students are required to use, all students in the class can benefit from your answer to a single student's question. If one student has a question, chances are good that many other students in the class are wondering the same thing. Yet you'll need to answer the question only once, and a written record of your answer will remain available online for all other students, at any future time, to reference.

Furthermore, an electronic bulletin board, if used well, can take some of the burden of answering questions off the individual instructor. Studies show that students learn much more effectively if they try to solve problems together, rather than asking the instructor for the answer. If you structure your class's use of an electronic bulletin board so that students see the benefits of peer collaboration, students can help one another with questions ranging from the simply administrative ("When is our midterm?") to the more analytically rigorous ("Can someone help me understand how to calculate K when one of the reactants is a solid?") Now that we have Blackboard on campus, it's quite simple to establish such bulletin boards, too.

You may be thinking that I'm crazy for recommending that you add yet one more mode of communicational technology, when the initial problem is actually a function of communicational technology. Think of it this way: each communicational medium has its own strengths and weaknesses, and it's our job as communicators to choose the most effective and efficient medium for various types of feedback. Instructor-student e-mail is very useful when private feedback is warranted. Devoting a few minutes of each class meeting to student questions, or establishing electronic bulletin boards, can help you reduce the number of e-mail questions you receive from students. Building small group activities in your course can encourage students to provide feedback to one another, rather than looking only to you for the answers.

Jonas

> **Quick Tip:** You should explain to your students that it is much easier, for both parties, if they ask technical questions, which involve complex formulas, in person during your office hours. The same is true for highly conceptual questions, which might require many pages of prose to ask and answer.

COMMUNICATING OUTSIDE OF CLASS

Dear **Jonas,**

Last week, I assigned a project to my class; the project was due today, Monday. Unfortunately, there was a typographical error that made the solution impossible in the last exercise and, apparently, none of the students discovered the anomaly until this past weekend. The students wasted lots of time working on an incorrectly written assignment, and I felt terrible. Of course, I had to give them an extension.

Obviously, I wish that I hadn't made a mistake on the assignment in the first place, but, given that I did, was there something I could have done to mollify the outcome? For future reference, I'd appreciate any suggestions that you have for communicating with students at times when I'm not in class or my office.

Typo Teacher

Dear **T-squared**,

Yes, those things happen - they've happened to me before - but, in the last few years, I've found that the Internet provides various means for me to keep in touch with my students at virtually any time.

Certainly, the easiest method of unobtrusive communication is via e-mail. Make sure that all of your students are aware of the fact that your e-mail address is on your syllabus. Encourage them to communicate with you via e-mail especially in situations as you described, and let them know how often you check your e-mail. Of course, in order to really help with the typo problem that you described, once a student notified you about the typo, you would have needed to e-mail all of your students about the issue. It's a good idea to ask your students for their e-mail addresses on the first day of class.

If you maintain your own Web page for your class, you can post class announcements there, including corrections to assignments. If you go this route, you should tell your students to consult your Web page on a routine basis, especially over weekends. If you had a chat area on your Web page, then you, yourself, would have been able to consult your Web page in order to learn about the typographical error.

Some instructors download instant messaging software

(AOL's Instant Messenger is very popular), and use it from home. They tell their students that they will be on-line from home at specified times, and are willing to have "electronic office hours". The instant messaging software is free, and allows for real-time, typed "conversations".

These Internet-based communications methods that I've described all require you to have Internet access from home. If this is not the case, you may want to consider telling your students that, in SOME situations, it is okay for them to call you at home; on the other hand, this option understandably makes many instructors a little uneasy. Another option is to encourage them to leave a message on your office voicemail, which you can agree to check on a daily basis.

The most important thing to remember is to be clear with yourself and your students about how and when you are available. While we want to respond to student needs as much as possible, we also want students to develop good time management skills and, therefore, we need to set appropriate limits as to our availability. If you really wish to be able to communicate with your students at odd times, and you don't want them calling you at home, the Internet is one way to go - if you don't have access, then I'd suggest that you've just provided yourself a darn good reason to get it. I wonder if the cost of the Internet connection would then be tax deductible? If someone knows for sure, please let me know, and I'll pass the information along.

Good luck,

Jonas

Quick Tip: To get your students' e-mail addresses the easy way, on the first day of class, ask each student to send you a one-sentence e-mail message containing his or her name, major, class, and year.

Chapter 6

Dear Jonas:

Since When Did I Become the Manager of the Class?

Thomas Sheahan

As college or university instructors, there is no doubt that we all experienced that defining moment early in our teaching careers when we faced our first disciplinary problem in class. Students in the back of the class disrupting what you thought was one of your most elegant lectures on a difficult concept, or that first time in class when you asked a question and a student responded with an answer that could not have been any more wrong. It was so wrong that most of the class either laughed or looked at you to see how you would handle the situation.

When we first become instructors, most of us are coming from a context that does little to prepare us for teaching undergraduates. Most new faculty have just finished graduate school or perhaps have worked in industry for some period of time. While some new faculty may have done some undergraduate instructor duty as teaching assistants, our last classroom experience was with reasonably mature, fellow graduate students who were fairly motivated toward learning. Issues such as discipline, civility toward an instructor, and cheating were generally not part of the classroom equation. In addition, we may have little or no experience (and therefore almost no level of comfort) with the kind of spontaneous, unrehearsed nature of student interactions in the classroom. Clearly, the easiest way to teach is to expound uninterrupted by student questions, or by asking questions to determine levels of understanding.

These issues are all part of the much less publicized role of the college instructor, that of the classroom "manager." We know about the instructor's important of role of "information (or knowledge) transmitter." But as classroom manager, we are responsible for handling and shaping students who are developing as learners, and we can best do this by communicating effectively with students. In this manager's role, instructors need to draw on the material covered in Chapters 5 (Communicating with Students) and 3 (Student Development).

The "Dear Jonas" column tackled the subjects in this chapter because they are some of the most challenging, and most pervasive, issues faced by college instructors. The first three columns on student behaviors (attendance, civility in the classroom and cheating) can be particular issues in freshman and sophomore classes when undergraduates are learning and testing the rules of the college classroom environment (the stage referred to as "moving in" by Tinto 1992; see Chapter 3). If any theme can be identified in these three columns, it is setting boundaries and expectations. When the column on cheating was written, we were facing a significant cheating scandal in one of the freshman science classes taken by first-year engineers. The following columns discuss changing and modifying expectations in the midst of the term. The next three columns on question-and-answer interactions in the classroom are applicable from freshman through graduate courses. While the "Dear Jonas" editors agreed that classroom Q & A interactions are heavily influenced by the instructor's personality and the size of the class, these interactions are incredibly important for student learning and instructor assessment of that learning; the literature on this issue confirms this. The next column in this chapter, on student-athletes, is again one of those issues that, if you haven't been on a varsity sports team, you may not be prepared to deal with. Like the first three columns, the one on student-athletes is about setting boundaries and expectations, but for a very specialized group of students. The last columns in this chapter discuss ways to collect and respond to students feedback on the course.

Classroom "management" presented in the literature is divided into structure/organization issues and faculty-student interactions. For example, Wulff (1988), Walvoord (1997) and Felder and Brent (1999) describe the contributions of organization and structure to teaching effectiveness. Gastel (1991) identified organization and clarity as two trademarks of highly effective teachers. Horvath (1980) provides a more detailed, itemized list of useful strategies for organizing a class and emphasizes "orderliness" in the class. This includes clearly stating policies on issues such as attendance, cheating, and expectations about in-class behavior. While much of Horvath's information is, as he acknowledges, common sense, it is a useful primer for beginning college instructors. Davidson and Ambrose (1994), in their list of eight principles of undergraduate education (an adaptation of those proposed by Chickering and Gamson 1987) include communicating high expectations, including attendance.

More actual research has been done on in-class faculty interactions, and their contribution to effective teaching. Tinto (1992) found that students do better academically (and are, as an important additional effect, more likely to persist) when they have quality interactions with faculty, including assessment mechanisms provided by in-class question-and-answer. The list of eight principles by Davidson and Ambrose (1994; noted earlier) includes encouraging active learning in the classroom, and encouraging student-faculty contact in the classroom. Karelis (1996) also identified the value of increased student-faculty communication and the benefits of ongoing assessment and feedback for students.

We can conclude that, as "Dear Jonas" emphasized in Chapter 5, effective student-faculty communication is perhaps the primary ingredient in effective teaching. In this chapter, this communication takes on the two forms of laying out boundaries and expectations, and having valuable in-class interactions. The first form of communication will help ensure the organization and orderly conduct of the class that frees the instructor to teach and the students to learn. The second form, particularly through question-and-answer interactions in the classroom, if done properly, yields a twofold benefit: it builds the rapport between the faculty and students that creates a more fruitful learning environment; and, it serves as an important, immediate assessment and feedback mechanism for faculty and students.

Further Reading

Books

1. Chickering, A. & Gameson, Z. (1987, March). *Seven Principles for Good Practice in Undergraduate Education.* AAHE Bulletin, 39:7, 3-7.

2. Davidson, C.I. and Ambrose, S.A. (1994). *The new professor's handbook: a guide to teaching and research in engineering and science.* Bolton, MA: Anker.

3. Horvath, R.J. (1980). Full classrooms: 95 practical suggestions to guarantee student and teacher success. In R.J. Horvath (Ed.), *The Handbook*, Louisville, KY: Jefferson Community College.

4. Tinto, V. (1992) *Student attrition and retention.* In B.R. Clark and G. R. Neave (Eds.), The Encyclopedia of Higher Education (Vol. 3, 1697-1709). Oxford: Pergamon Press.

Presentations

1. Felder, R.M. and Brent, R. (1999). *Effective Teaching: A Workshop*. Workshop presented at the 1999 Civil Engineering Conference and Exposition, Charlotte, NC.

2. Karelis, C.H. (1996). *Lessons learned from FIPSE projects III*. Washington, DC: U.S. Dept. of Education.

3. Walvoord, B.E. (1997). Presentation at the Center for Instructional Development and Research, University of Washington, Seattle, WA.

4. Wulff, D.H. (1988). *Case studies of the communication of effective university instructors*. Paper presented at the Annual Meeting of the Speech Communication Association, New Orleans, LA.

Websites

1. 24 Making Classroom Attendance Mandatory. (Crimson & Gold) Office of University Advancement & Marketing for alumni and friends of the University. Ferris State University. http://www.ferris.edu/htmls/alumni/c&g/dec98/homepage.html

2. Kerkvlist, J. and Sigmund, C. L. (1999) Can We Control Cheating in the Classroom? *The Journal of Economic Education*.
http://susan.uits.indiana.edu/jeeJeeArtilceSearch_VOpenFile.cfm?serverFilePath=D%3A%5 CInetpub%5Cwwwroot%5CJEE%5Cpdffiles%5Cfall99%5Ckerkvliet%2Epdf

3. Mazur, E. Peer Instruction: Collaborative learning in large lectures. Harvard University. Mazur Group. http://mazur-www.harvard.edu/research/detailspage.php?ed=1&rowid=8

---

4. Asking Good Classroom Questions. Ball State University. http://www.bsu.edu/burris/iwonder/strategies/questions.html

ATTENDANCE

Dear **Jonas**,

As the spring semester progresses, I am finding that attendance in my classes is a problem. Out of a class of 30 students it is not unusual for 6 to 8 to be missing. These students then want to know what they missed, and providing these overviews has become very time consuming for me. They also want to hand in assignments late and they request makeup work. It seems to be getting out of hand. What do you recommend?

Lonely in the Classroom

Dear Lonely,

I try to be proactive in the classroom to address this behavior early. I try to explain the responsibility that students have for their own learning and tell them that coming to class is the students' job. It is their responsibility to attend, and should be considered a commitment. Although many of the students are freshmen, I compare it to an internship or job: if they were not going to work on any given day, I discuss what they would do, such as, call the boss, email the boss, etc. However, if you really want to require attendance, then consider instituting an attendance policy on the syllabus, which you could stress in the first class and review with them periodically during the quarter.

There are a number of policies that encourage attendance or provide consequences for lack of attendance. Some encouraging policies include: attendance as a percentage of the course grade, bonus points or extra credit for good attendance. Some policies that involve consequences include: points deducted for a certain number of missed classes or grade reductions by certain percentages, based on the number of classes missed. I tell my students that of course I allow excused absences, but they need to provide a Doctor's written note for the missed classes to be counted as excused.

You do not appear to have an attendance policy, so at this juncture; some discussion with the whole class can be helpful. You can remind the students about their responsibilities as I discussed above. Or, if you know all of the students by name, you can acknowledge that they are missed when they are not there, and give positive feedback when they are. This is, of course, easier with small class sizes. In larger classes you can try in-class assignments, one-minute reflections, or other ways to check attendance, and follow up individually when non-attendance is a problem. I also try to keep variety in my classes, to keep them dynamic, to let the students know what is coming up, so that they are motivated to attend the next class. If I am excited to be there and looking forward to it, and genuinely disappointed when they are not there, they follow suit. Of course, we all have had Spring Fever.

Jonas

> **Quick Tip:** Have students bring in one question about the homework and collect their questions at each class. You can answer them in class or post the answers on your class web page.

CHANGING THE GROUND RULES

Dear **Jonas,**

My course syllabus stated that we would have two "midterm" exams this term, each counting as 20% towards the course grade, with homework and projects counting as another 20%, and the final exam counting as the remaining 40%. This term, I gave the first midterm a little later than I had intended, and I've gotten slightly behind the syllabus in presenting the material. Now I see that this term is a week shorter

---

than the Fall term; I don't see how I can fit in the second midterm exam. I told the class these things, and that I wanted to cancel the second midterm. I told them that I would count everything else proportionately greater. This seemed to elicit a strong reaction from many students, and several of them told me after class that they thought that changing the grading policy at this point was unfair.

Is it really so bad to change the way in which I calculate the students' grades? Shouldn't I be allowed to change my grading policy to adapt to the course's progress?

Midterm Blues Man

Dear **Blues Man,**

While instructors get behind in their syllabi for a variety of reasons, I'm afraid that I think the students' objections are justified. It is important for instructors to check the academic calendar before preparing their testing and grading schemes. The testing/grading policy listed on the syllabus and given to your students on the first day of class is a contract between you and your students. While that contract may not be a type that is legally binding (I'm not an attorney, but my daughter plays one on TV), it is certainly morally binding, and students base a number of decisions and expectations on the stated grading policy. The establishment of a trusting relationship between you and your students is also injured. Effective time management is an important steppingstone to success in a student's academic life. Our students are constantly making decisions about how much work to put into each of their courses on any given day. Right or wrong, when studying for that first midterm exam, or when working on homework and projects, a number of your students may have decided to devote more time to some other course knowing they still had the second midterm exam to fall back on. It is impossible for students to make appropriate time management decisions if their instructors change the ground rules as the term progresses.

To put things in perspective, imagine how you yourself would feel, or would have felt, if halfway through your tenure-track period, your department or the University told you that the way in which they would evaluate your past and future accomplishments had been changed. Not only would you be uncertain where you stood at the moment, but also you would worry that perhaps the procedure would change yet again in the future.

Some faculty members believe that changing the grading policy is okay, as long as it is a change that clearly cannot result in lower student grades. An example of this would be to announce at the end of the term that you will give each student the better of two grades: the grade earned only on the final exam or the grade calculated according to the originally stated policy. While instructors sometimes implement this sort of change, you should still be careful - you don't want to be unfair to those students who worked hard to do well according to the original scheme.

I understand that it will be difficult for you to fit in that second midterm exam, but it will be more difficult for your students to deal with a shifting grading policy. You need to find the time to give that second exam, at least in some form. Perhaps you could consider giving a take-home test, or maybe shortening the midterm exam to half of a class period.

Jonas

> **Quick Tip:** One way to "change" your grading policy to help students who are doing poorly is by giving optional quizzes or tests, which some students may take and others may skip unpenalized. This is a good device, for it leaves your grading policy unchanged for those who opt out of taking

the test, while still not being unfair by simply boosting the grades of the others.

CHANGING THE SYLLABUS MIDSTREAM

Dear **Jonas,**

In your last column, you wrote about changing the syllabus in the middle of the term. At one point, you mentioned that while the syllabus may not be legally binding, it is "morally binding." I've spoken with some colleagues who are of the opinion that the original syllabus virtually does have the status of a legal contract between instructor and students. Others maintain that, if the changes won't adversely affect student grades, it's o.k. Can you give any more guidance on this?

Worried Syllabus Slider

Dear **Worried,**

Obviously, most instructors are not lawyers (nor am I), so we shouldn't be expected to write our syllabi like contracts that must be followed to the letter for fear that students would hold us "liable" for breaching its terms. The syllabus would wind up reading like a mortgage agreement! Clearly then, I view the syllabus as a moral agreement rather than a legal one, and moral agreements bring more responsibility rather than less. It may be a matter of semantics, but I would prefer to think of the syllabus as a firm "handshake" agreement that you make with your students about the guidelines that will govern how both the instructor and student will conduct themselves. It is up to each instructor to be as specific or as general as he or she would like. However, in my experience, a more complete, detailed syllabus yields a smoother and less contentious operation. It will result in fewer questions and fewer attempts by students to see "loopholes" in the syllabus. These loopholes might undermine achieving your learning objectives, or the effectiveness of your grading policy and office hours, as well as other expectations that you have for the course and the students.

So, having said this, what about the instructor changing the syllabus in the middle of the academic term? Can you make changes without students claiming that you have breached or contradicted some part of the contract or syllabus agreement? In the earlier Jonas column, I voiced my objections to making changes, particularly to the grading policy. I likened this to changing the rules for the tenure process midway through the evaluation period. I still think that this is valid.

In my mind, there is one overarching rule for syllabus changes: any modifications must hold the students harmless as a result of the change. Examples of the kinds of "harm" that could result include: a student in the class would be required to do extra work beyond that described in the original syllabus; a student would be put at a disadvantage compared to other students in the class with regard to their grades or workload; changes in grading policy would lead to a lower grade for a student than under the original grading plan; or, changes in office hours would give students less access to you for help. Clearly, you can modify the syllabus where the language is ambiguous to clear up legitimate questions about a policy or topic coverage. But substantive changes should be carefully considered and discussed with the class before they are implemented. An honest discussion with students about why you want to make a particular change, and how it might impact their grades, workload, etc. will go a long way to alleviate potential anxieties about the changes. They may not say it, but you can be sure that they will appreciate that you respect them enough to have had the discussion and sought their opinions.

So the bottom line is that mid-term syllabus changes should not be made lightly or frequently. However, if you feel strongly that a modification is needed, make it after discussion with the class, and ensure that no student will be harmed by the changes.

Jonas

Quick Tip: To read more about components of and considerations that go into creating effective syllabi, see the extensive on-line University of Minnesota Syllabus Tutorial at: www1.umn.edu/ohr/teachlearn/syllabus/index.html.

CIVILITY IN THE CLASSROOM

Dear **Jonas,**

Help me! This is the first year that I've taught, and I'm not happy with some of the behaviors in my class this quarter and am not sure what to do. The problems range from students wearing hats and shorts, and eating and drinking in class, to students who are disruptive and say improper things to me and to other students. I've tried ignoring the problems and I've tried the other extreme, calling disruptive students on their behavior in class, but things are only getting worse. What can I do?

Intimidated Instructor

Dear **Intimidated,**

This is an increasingly common issue in higher education classes so take heart you're not the only one. I believe that I could type for pages on this question, but I'll try to be brief. I'm going to tell you my thoughts on the matter, and

---

what works for me and for other professors I talk to.

As you've noticed, ignoring disciplinary problems tends to lead to more problems, and yelling at a given student frequently only serves to make him/her angry and defensive in return.

Here are some suggestions I use. First of all, I try to treat my students as I would treat my colleagues in similar circumstances. If my colleagues are attending a meeting or seminar and are late, leave early, have a cell phone ring, bring lunch with them, etc., I try to understand that people have other commitments, that people forget to turn off phones, and that people sometimes have trouble fitting a meal into their day. As long as students come and go quietly, look appropriately embarrassed at a cell phone ringing, and eat quietly while paying attention, I treat them like adults and don't object.

However, I believe that joking comments - like one might make to a colleague - are appropriate. Something along the lines of, "Nice of you to drop in" for a student who comes in significantly late might be in order. It lets the student know that you've noticed his/her tardiness, but it does so in a non-confrontational manner. In addition, if a given student is constantly early or late to class, you should talk to them (calmly) after class, and try to find out if there is some legitimate reason for their unusual activities. Try to keep in mind, though, that if you're going to object to students being tardy or leaving early, then it is only reasonable for you to be careful to end your class on time.

For students who are constantly talking and being disruptive, I try humorous comments the first couple of times, then I try a stern (but still calm), serious comment about how other students are trying to learn - this never fails. Other colleagues have walked the aisle and stand near the students talking while they continue class. Some professors raise the disruption as a class issue and ask students for their input on how to deal with their disruptive classmates.

As for matters of politeness, such as not wearing hats or shorts in class, I believe that these are a matter of taste, and that some students will seriously object to such rules. Sometimes it's a matter of degree - on a hot spring day, I once had a male student attend class without a shirt on; if I had yelled at him, I think there would have been a protracted argument. What I did do was to laughingly suggest that perhaps his shirtlessness was "a bit much", and he put his shirt on while making some joking comment back.

However, if you wish to set certain expectations in your classroom, you need to make them clear on the first day and in your syllabus. I think it would help to point out that there will be such rules later in the workplace and there are also such rules at many nightclubs - so it's not that unreasonable for you to have a dress-code, or other rules of decorum, in your class.

As for improper things that students might say to you, you can try to brush them off in an amused fashion. Whatever you do, do not respond in kind. If it is a frequent problem with one student, you should talk to him/her outside of class, as inappropriate or rude behavior does not need to be tolerated. On the other hand, I have a different attitude when it comes to one student making an offensive comment to another student in front of the whole class. This is the only time when I believe that the correct response is to tell the offending student that personal attacks are never appropriate or tolerated in your class; the general populace in your class needs to know in no uncertain terms that you will not tolerate students abusing other students.

I said that I would try to be brief, but the list of strategies for keeping control of a class is endless. My comments above boil down to: establish classroom expectations from the beginning, try to deal with problems that don't affect other students in a humorous fashion, and deal with problems that do affect the other students in a serious manner.

Jonas

> **Quick Tip:** When some students are chatting and not paying attention, continue your class but walk up the aisle and stand by them for a while. They'll quiet down.

CHEATING

Dear **Jonas,**

I'm trying to work through a frustrating experience. I gave an exam to my freshman class yesterday and finished grading it late last night. When I got to my office this morning I had a call from someone in the Student Services Office who wanted to give me a heads-up. She told me that a few of my students had stopped by to complain that some others in the class were cheating during the exam. Even though she urged the students to speak directly with me, they indicated that they wouldn't. I'm upset about the cheating. I'm upset that the students who observed it don't want to talk to me about it, and I'm upset that I didn't detect it.

Not Sherlock Holmes

Dear **Dr. Watson,**

I understand your frustration; we would like to think that everyone around us would behave in a highly ethical manner. Unfortunately, as we are too often reminded, there are always some who cross ethical boundaries. Don't be overly concerned that students are reluctant to approach you about issues like this; they are not yet the mature decision-makers that most will become by graduation.

In the short run, there's not much you can do about the current situation without proof. You could review the exam solutions with an eye toward looking for evidence of cheating (e.g., unlikely identical solutions, identical misspellings, unlikely identical names for variables, wrong work but right answer, etc.). Hidden notes (cheat sheets) are long gone.

Diligence in preventing and detecting cheating takes effort that we'd rather invest elsewhere. Perhaps I'm wrong, but I have the sense from your letter that you feel you weren't as diligent as you might have been. Setting appropriate expectations and environments are critical. Some questions might provide a guide. Is there a statement about academic honesty on your syllabus? If so, is it clearly and constructively stated to reflect your expectations for ethical behavior and society's expectations of engineers' behavior in general? Did you restate your expectations prior to the exam? Were there obstacles presented by the exam setting? Was the room too congested? If so (and a better one wasn't available), did you prepare a couple of different versions of the exam? Was there adequate attentive supervision throughout the exam? While no one enjoys a prisoner camp environment, students do appreciate measures that insure fairness.

Distasteful as it might be, my last comment focuses on the critical issue of dealing with offenders when detected. Don't be a vigilante; bring the situation to the attention of the Judicial Affairs Office for advice. They are set up to adjudicate, to issue fair findings/punishment and to keep appropriate records. Quite often, a first offense is punished by a grade of zero on the work involved, disciplinary probation, etc. A second offense (indiscernible if there is no official record of a first offense) typically results in suspension or expulsion.

Unfortunately, there will always be those who try to cheat. Equally unfortunate is that we must invest the effort to prevent, detect and report cheating.

Jonas

WHY ASK QUESTIONS

Dear **Jonas:**

In a recent column, you recommended that faculty break up lectures with other activities. I understand that some of my colleagues stop their lectures to ask questions of the students as part of their lesson. Doesn't it seem contrived? Also it's very time-consuming. Wouldn't my time be better spent covering the material?

Questioning questions

Dear **Questioning**:

Asking the students questions in class is actually a very effective and efficient teaching tool. It does not have to seem contrived, in fact, it can wake up the class! In addition, quality feedback from students can actually help you use class time more efficiently by allowing you to focus on areas where students have difficulties. There are several ways that questions can be used as tools for learning. These include providing the professor with a quick assessment of the students' understanding of the subject material, giving students an opportunity to apply the material, and helping students make connections to previous knowledge.

As a professor, you may want to ascertain students' comprehension of a concept that you consider a building block for a new topic that you are about to introduce. Asking questions can help you gauge what students already know or don't know, and how well they actually understand the concept. After a concept or operation has been introduced, you can ask application questions to get feedback on how well the students grasped the material. For example, after you've introduced some basic notions of probability theory, you could ask a student how this applies to the Massachusetts State Lottery. If they can't apply the concept, then you know they really haven't understood the concept and only followed the mechanics. Some more specific questioning might point you to the cause of the problem, and provide you with the opportunity to clarify. Additionally, asking questions based on the material just presented provides students with feedback on whether they understand and can apply the information correctly.

Often, particularly in the sciences and engineering, lessons focus on operations and application of theory. A question, often in the form of a quick problem or part of a problem, gives students practice applying these operations immediately. This is a powerful tool for reinforcing instruction. By giving the students an opportunity to be active learners and engage their minds, they become physically active and test out their new knowledge, allowing real learning to happen. Well-constructed questions can focus their attention on the key points that you are trying to make, as well as change the rhythm of the lesson. Studies have shown that a change in presentation style every 20 minutes maximizes attention.

Finally, questions can help students integrate knowledge and form links with prior learning and experience. Asking for analogies, similar situations, or connections to previous ideas facilitates retention of new information, and allows students to make connections with what they already know. So questioning - as part of your lesson - is an effective teaching tool and a way to gain information about what the students are learning. What are your questions now?

Jonas

> **Quick Tip:** To see how the students are doing, I often ask them to tell me where the concept or operation would apply. Have they seen it before or used anything similar before? What does it remind them of? That way I know that the application is one that they are familiar with, and that it ties to something they have seen or known before, without giving applications or examples myself.

ASKING QUESTIONS: HOW TO

Dear **Jonas,**

I read with anticipation your recent column about asking students questions in class. I am willing to spend some class time to get students actively engaged in what I want them to learn and to get some feedback on whether or not they "get it". I have tried using questions or short exercises for students, but I have not found a really effective way to do this. Sometimes, I get no response and when I do get a response, it is usually from the same two or three students. I sense that their feedback is not representative of the rest of the class. Worse, I am concerned that the majority of the class is just waiting for others to respond, which defeats the main purpose of asking the question in the first place. Are there more effective ways to use in-class questioning?

Inquiet Inquisitor

Dear **I. I.,**

I am glad to see that you want to encourage your students to adopt a "minds-on" approach to what you want them to learn, and appreciate the frustration of getting blank stares.

You're right - research shows that (1) the type of question asked, (2) the manner in which the question is posed, and (3) the amount of time an instructor waits for an answer all influence the effectiveness of in-class questions.

Some instructors have success with randomly selecting students to answer questions. To make this effective, let the students know up front that you will be "cold-calling", and try to alleviate any anxiety about not knowing the correct answer. Students don't want to appear stupid in front of their classmates. If you have developed good rapport and set class expectations that questioning is a way to sharpen thinking, then the possibility of being called on may motivate most students to consider your question carefully. If the same few students are participating, it is a good idea to target before asking the next question: "Someone I haven't heard from yet today..." When you want to ascertain that specific concepts are coming across, try posing a multiple-choice question. This ensures that students will understand exactly what you're trying to get at. Rather than asking "What happens when you mix A and B?", you might ask "When solid A reacts with liquid B, the reaction vessel will (a) heat up, (b) cool down, (c) stay the same temperature, or (d) explode and obliterate the entire building." This approach avoids wasting class time on irrelevant answers (e.g., "it turns blue"), and can be applied in classes of almost any size. A class of 100 students can be polled in 15 seconds by a show of hands. Again, if you want a more detailed response and it feels comfortable, you could follow up by asking one or two individual students to (briefly) explain the choices they made.

Try to word questions carefully. If you expect something other than a multiple-choice answer, be specific about what you're looking for - a hand-sketched graph? a short verbal explanation? a number?. An ambiguous question is not as disastrous in class as it would be on an exam, but if it happens very often students may become reluctant to respond.

Consider preparing questions ahead of time on transparencies, as this forces you to consider your wording.

Be sure to allow sufficient wait time! Students realize very quickly when an instructor becomes uncomfortable with silence and jumps in with the answer. Studies have shown that students need time to realize that a question has been asked, to process what the question is, to come up with an answer, and to get the courage to raise their hands. Allowing a pause as short as 5-10 seconds has been shown to increase student response if the question is posed clearly.

If you run a class where students are expected to participate, consider establishing that from the first class meeting. Rather than spending the session reading the syllabus for them, or lecturing about some topic, you might break them into groups and give them a short problem or project to work on. This sends the message right away that this is the kind of course where they will be expected to think, talk, and answer questions.

Effective questioning can actively engage students in their own learning, by continually challenging them to apply newly introduced concepts while they are fresh in their minds. The resulting feedback allows the instructor to adjust the pace and content of the class in real time. Better questioning by teachers equals sharper thinking by students!

Jonas

Quick Tip 1: To increase student engagement, you might consider counting student responses as part of the course grade or as bonus points. As long as the weight in the overall course grade is small, this can increase student involvement without undue anxiety.

Quick tip 2: Try "peer instruction" method by Eric Mazur, at Harvard. In Mazur's classes, students are first asked to consider a question and polled. Then they are invited to discuss the answer with other students for a stated period (usually 1-2 min) and polled again. Mazur's data show that the fraction of correct responses increases significantly after discussion with classmates, suggesting that effective peer instruction takes place during the discussion period.

REACTING TO STUDENT RESPONSES

Dear **Jonas,**

I read the last two letters on asking questions, and I have been diligently using questions more frequently in my classes. It is generally going pretty well, though it started slowly, I think because they weren't used to it. My problem is their responses to my questions. I know they aren't stupid - they are doing well on my quizzes, but you can't tell that from their answers. If I tell them that their answer is wrong, it seems to just clam up that person, and the rest of the class. How do I handle those responses that are just wrong, off-track, or just ridiculous?

Diligent Questionner

Dear **D. Q.,**

The way students perceive your responses to questions are very important, and have a critical effect on students' anxiety. They do not want to be wrong and embarrass themselves before their peers. Even if the answer seems dead wrong, every student should be encouraged even if just for trying. Here's one way to do this. After listening very carefully, and in an unhurried way, select some part of the answer that was insightful or creative to reinforce their effort. For example, a student might respond to the question, "How do we determine the required sample size for this problem?" with "Take as many as you can." You might then smile and say "Yes, that is true, a good thought in the right direction because more samples provide more accuracy, but that can get expensive. Can we use the desired accuracy to calculate the sample size needed, any thoughts on that?" In this way, you reward a student for trying, and you can highlight something positive about their contribution. You may have to reinterpret things rather creatively to accomplish this. You might respond by asking the class if others agree or not with the initial student response and elicit more responses.

The class is watching closely to see if the instructor displays an accepting attitude. That is why the whole class seems to "clam up" when they perceive a less than friendly reaction to student responses. It is more critical to respond carefully to wrong answers than to the brilliant ones in communicating this accepting attitude.

Nonverbal messages are also crucial in influencing the atmosphere after answering questions. You have to be very vigilant and self-controlled so as to not be scowling or throwing up your hands after a "stupid" or frustrating answer. If you sigh or look away, you are also sending negative nonverbal messages. You should make eye contact with the student, possibly lean towards him/her, to display an attitude while answering. Other nonverbal cues are smiling and nodding as they answer, to affirm your interest. However, don't be afraid to point out clearly that an answer is wrong. One of six top non-facilitating teaching behaviors (Napell, 1976) is automatically rewarding the first answer. The key to mastering this fine line is HOW your respond. Saying "Wrong!" is different from saying "Thanks for taking a stab at it, but that's not right" and then using the techniques above, to lead the student to the right answer.

Be prepared to provide some feedback to the students about their responses to survey-type questions. For example, multiple-choice questions are most effective if there are wrong answers that look attractive to students who make common conceptual errors. Take the opportunity to point out these errors, but be gentle, e.g., "those of you who chose answer 2 were at least half right, because you recognized that..., but those of you who chose the correct answer 5, also realized that..." One common outcome of well-chosen questions is that they can elicit follow-up student questions that are more focused and concrete than the "explain it again" variety that come up when you simply pause to ask "are there any questions?"

Good questions and answers can help a class become quite active and engaging for everyone. I applaud you for trying and encourage you to keep it up. It is a very effective way to see what students are learning and have learned and to keep the class lively and engaged. Good luck with your creative responses to some very creative answers.

Jonas

Quick Tip: To encourage a hesitant class to answer questions, you can pair them up, or team them up quickly to formulate answers, and then you can ask the group what they came up with. This is less threatening and can really loosen up the class if responses are not forthcoming.

STUDENT ATHLETES

Dear **Jonas,**

Recently, a first-year engineering student who had been absent for one of my classes came to my office hours to tell me that it was because of a special conference tournament her team had played in. She's on the women's basketball team, and this tournament was a post-season event. As a result, she had missed an important review for the final, and she's already struggling. My discipline requires a lot of time and effort. I feel that students in this field need to make a choice - either their academics come first, or they should re-consider their major. I suggested that perhaps she couldn't be a student and a varsity athlete. She seemed very upset when I said this. What are my responsibilities in this case? I find it frustrating that I'm supposed to help her when she misses class like this.

A Lacking Sports Sympathizer

Dear **Lacking**,

Although they're often mislabeled as "dumb jocks," the fact is that student-athletes regularly succeed in a number of very challenging majors at our university. In many cases, student-athletes have a higher graduation rate than non-athletes in their peer group. These students have to be extremely motivated to be both good in their academic pursuits and meet the demands of whatever team they're on. They also have to be better-than-average time managers to juggle classes, labs, and recitations with practices, team meetings and travel to away games. However, like most students, student-athletes are learning how to manage their time without the help of parents, and with the additional responsibilities that come with living away from home (for example, buying groceries, doing their laundry, etc.). In addition to these pressures, it is likely that student-athletes who are on a scholarship perceive their athlete status as the only way they can afford to go to school. A similar kind of pressure exists for students who have to work a lot of hours to support themselves while attending school. All of this is a lot of pressure for an18 or 19 year-old.

According to the university's student handbook, students are allowed to miss class for an intercollegiate athletic event, and faculty are required to provide assistance in making up for that class. However, the student should learn from this experience. If this situation were to occur again, she should e-mail or call all of the professors whose classes are impacted by the athletic event as soon as she knew about it, and explain the situation. This can reduce misunderstanding between faculty members and the student and allow some time for you to consider how she can best make up the material missed. Additionally she could have arranged to get the notes for the class from another student or two, gone over them and then met with you with any questions. Since the student is struggling in your class, you could have talked with her about her study habits. Ask about the amount of time she is putting into your class assignments, quiz and exam preparation, etc. Is she working in a study group, or trying to go it alone? Does she know about any on-campus tutoring resources? Has she sought help from the support services for student athletes? These are all worthwhile questions to ask not only this student, but also all students who come to you because they're struggling. Again, it's important for students to learn that success is facilitated if they identify problems early, make appropriate decisions and take timely action to resolve these problems. The University, Colleges, and in many cases, your department has a number of resources to help students. We should encourage students to use those resources when they need help.

In addition to encouraging the student to seek help from other sources, you can provide some assistance. For instance, you can encourage her to come to office hours, or make an appointment to see you for some help. This is not to repeat the entire lecture, but for the student to get any questions answered or help after she's reviewed other students' notes. I have found that a small amount of time and effort goes a long way with these motivated students.

Jonas

> **Quick Tip:** If you have a varsity athlete in your class, you'll receive a student-athlete academic progress form to fill out during the quarter. Be sure to fill this out and return it promptly.

MIDTERM ASSESSMENT

Dear **Jonas**,

In both of the classes that I'm teaching, I have a sort of uneasy feeling that the students just aren't getting much out of class. They sit there very quietly every day, only speaking when directly called upon. When I ask if I'm covering the material too quickly or slowly, if they're finding the course difficult, how they like the textbook, or simply how things are going in the class in general, they respond with unenthusiastic "okay's or "fine's.

Maybe the classes really are okay, but I'm not sure. How can I get some more constructive feedback from my students?

Uneasy Instructor

Dear **Uneasy**,

I understand your plight. I think that anyone who has taught for a number of years has had classes like yours, classes that just don't feel right, and most of us have experienced the struggle involved in convincing students that we really would appreciate constructive criticism.

However, the good news is that there are fairly simple, effective mechanisms for obtaining constructive feedback from your classes: the one-minute paper and a midterm assessment form (MAF).

The one-minute paper is a quick, simple way to get ongoing feedback about the class. The technique is simple. At the end of class, you ask students to answer a couple simple questions anonymously on a 3x5 card. For example, you might ask: (1) what was the main idea/concept/operation you learned today, (2) what questions do you still have about today's class and/or (3) what feedback do you have for the instructor. You can do this after every class, once a week, or whenever you feel it's necessary. This will allow you to "have your finger on the pulse" of the class and make timely adjustments where necessary.

An MAF is a short document, which you distribute to your classes around the middle of the term; it is a formative document meant to provide the type of feedback that can help shape the class for the remainder of the term. Typically, one would take ten minutes at the end of one class, hand out the MAF's, wait for the students to finish them, collect the forms, and read them almost immediately. It is extremely important to inform the students beforehand as to exactly what the MAF is, and to be clear that you are going to read their comments immediately. It is also important, after reading the MAF's, to clarify questions you have and tell the students about any course changes that you plan to make as a result of their comments. I have attached two sample midterm assessment forms of different types, one open-ended from Professor Sue Freeman, one in a check off/short reply format from Dr. Miriam Diamond. You may wish to use one of these, or you can create your own. If you create your own, I suggest that you keep it short and simple.

For more comprehensive mid-term feedback you may want to contact the Teaching Center. They have a mid-semester feedback program called Small Group Instructional Diagnosis (SGID). The Teaching Center staff will come into your class around mid-term and take the students through a half-hour 4-step process to gather feedback and then meet with you and discuss the results. This process is particularly helpful if you feel that there are conflicting student expectations for the class, because this process forces students to talk to each other and to discuss the student role in the learning process. Perhaps some of the questions on this SGID form would be appropriate to use if you create your own midterm assessment form.

Finally, I should make it clear that an MAF has a different purpose than the standard evaluation forms, which we distribute near the end of the term; evaluations are summative documents intended to rate the instructor and the course. The midterm assessment forms are totally different - they are designed solely to help the instructor make mid-course corrections.

Jonas

> **Quick Tip:** Try one of these forms in the middle of the term!

Northeastern University

Mid-Term Feedback Form

To what extent does your instructor:	Very much	Somewhat	Not at all	Comments
1. convey information clearly?				
2. motivate you to do good work?				
3. provide sufficient examples of concepts?				
4. use visual aids effectively?				
5. encourage class participation?				
6. help when students are confused?				
7. effectively answer student questions?				
8. make themselves accessible for meetings and office hours?				
9. demonstrate respect to students?				
10. make best use of class time available?				

11. What most helps my learning in this class is:

12. What most hinders my learning in this class is:

13. What the instructor can do to help me learn this material better:

14. What I can do to improve my learning in this class:

Northeastern University
Engineering Course
Mid-term Feedback/Assessment Form

Instructor: _____ Course: _____

1. What do you like about the course? This can be class exercises, homework, books, projects, lectures, and/or other aspects of the course.

2. What would you change about the course, what suggestions for improvement do you have?

3. How would you summarize the course for someone who asked you what the course is about? Be brief.

5. Summarize what you feel you have learned so far in this course.

Thank you!

_____

END-OF-TERM COURSE EVALUATION RESULTS

Dear Jonas,

I just received the summary of my Teacher-Course Evaluations for a course I taught last term, and I must admit to being a bit confused. Let me give you some information. It was a required course taught to first-term sophomore engineers and was the first major-specific course in the curriculum (they're taking another at the same time). Overall the ratings were OK - 4.2 out of 5.0 on teaching effectiveness with a standard deviation of 0.7. Of the 39 students who completed the evaluation forms, nine wrote comments about "What has the instructor done especially well in this course?" and eight had comments for "What suggestions would you make to improve this course section?"

How do I reconcile comments such as: "He is always prepared for class and does all he can do to make sure we understand the material, very effective!" with "Teach in a more understandable manner."?

Another conflicting set of comments read: "Emphasized importance of material in engineering career. Treated students like adults, rewards those who put in effort" but "He talks to the class like they are in elementary school and is sometimes rude".

The remainder of the suggested improvement comments revolved around how much credit should be allowed for homework performance. What do I do with such contradictory comments?

Mixed Message City

Dear **Mixed,**

It is very common to receive conflicting feedback. There are a few issues to keep in mind when reviewing TCEP reports, so I will address some of the common perceptions, provide suggestions for improvement, and discuss the use of TCEP trends over time.

I operate under the premise that student scores and comments are honest reflections of their perceptions. In a sense, there is an analogy with SAT scores that helps me to maintain perspective. While an average SAT score for a large cohort (e.g., an entering freshman class) is a strong predictor of the average success rate (e.g., graduation rate), the SAT score for any particular individual is not anywhere nearly as good a predictor of that individual's success (especially as the standard deviation becomes larger). Similarly, one person's perception is not necessarily the last word on your teaching.

With an average score of 4.2 on teaching effectiveness and a standard deviation of 0.7, your students have uniformly perceived your overall efforts as quite effective, especially as this is a required course. The distribution of the comments the students made was also roughly reflective of that kind of numerical distribution. However, without being present in your class, I can't reconcile the comment about treating students like adults with the one about treating them as if they were in elementary school. I can only say that by taking a figurative "average" of the comments you noted, the "elementary school" one does not seem to be a perception shared by others. I guess I would simply make a mental note that someone perceived my efforts in a way that was not what I would have wanted; however, since no examples were given, I won't dwell on it.

I would spend more time thinking about another set of comments though. You did mention that a number of the comments in the "improvement" category addressed the amount of credit you give for homework performance. Since there is some consistency here (something of a trend, if you will), this bears more attention. I would think about these comments in two ways. First, should I give more credit for homework? Second, even if I decided not to give more credit, perhaps I should make more of an effort on my syllabus and in class to describe the logic that underlies my grading scheme. The bottom line is that I would use the evaluations in a formative way to improve my classroom presentation for the next term.

What I look for in TCEP comments and ratings is trends over time. Everyone has a difficult quarter or class at one time or other and TCEP scores reflect that. I chart my TCEP rating and comments each quarter for my own use. If I see that a score is lower than I would like, or that there is a set of recurring comments for 3 out of 5 quarters, then I know there is something here I have to look at seriously.

I also use TCEP scores and comments to determine if I might want some peer feedback on my teaching the next quarter, especially if I'm perplexed by a low score or a series of comments. Student comments, as I stated earlier, are perceptual. You often need another perspective, other than student opinions, to get a true picture of what is happening in your class.

Don't forget that results of other questions on the back of the TCE form might also provide useful information and shouldn't be ignored, such as providing an estimate of how much time individuals are devoting to your class and how useful they find the text.

To get the full picture of your teaching, I recommend using evaluations, mid-term feedbacks, and peer feedbacks collected over time.

Jonas

Quick Tip: Save your TCEP reports - organized by course and term - for future reference to note trends and progress. You will also need them for your teaching portfolio in tenure and promotion reviews.

Chalk Talk – E-advice from Jonas Chalk

Chapter 7

Dear Jonas:

How Can I Be Everything to Everybody?

Donna M. Qualters

Every semester we face two constants in the classroom: the excitement of meeting new students with their varied backgrounds, personalities, needs, and interests; and the challenge of meeting new students with their varied backgrounds personalities, needs, and interests. Diversity, in all its forms, is one of the most significant challenges faced by classroom teachers in an ever increasing global world. Our students are diverse in where they come from, how they learn, what they know, and why they are in our course. As teachers, we are faced with honoring that diversity while at the same time juggling the demands that those differences require of us in our teaching preparation and practice.

As teachers, we struggle with differences in knowledge base, especially with freshmen who come to us from so many different educational experiences. We often feel we are faced with slowing down the instruction at the risk of loosing the more academically prepared or letting those without the necessary prior knowledge find their own way of gaining the pre-requisite information. We struggle with diversity in the way people learn. Research has extensively documented the existence of various learning styles and their impact on learning (Kolb & Fry, 1975; Dunn, 2000; Gardner, 1983). We often have students in front of us who do not learn the way we do and have not been taught the way we teach. It then becomes clear that unless we try to enter into their world and think of different approaches to stimulate everyone's learning these students may not succeed. It is also beneficial for the learners if teachers try to find ways to help students adapt their learning styles. Recent research has shown that learning to think is different in the different disciplines (Donald, 2002) yet our experience and knowledge is grounded in *our* particular discipline and we are unfamiliar with ways to provide for this difference in classes where students come from a variety of math, science, and professional fields. We also face classes where the student population can be racially, ethnically and economically different from our personal experience. Since much of teaching draws from that experience, we do not have a lens in which to view our students' world. Lastly, with the adoption of the Americans with Disabilities Act and the advancements in technology, students with documented disabilities are now able to avail themselves of higher education in much greater numbers than ever before. Again, as teachers inexperienced in these areas, the use of adaptive technology, universal design, and interpreters can be an unfamiliar intrusion into our comfortable class routine.

While each of these differences poses challenges to even the most seasoned instructor, it also creates frustration. That frustration is echoed in the Jonas columns in this chapter. We have found that our colleagues want to be the best they can in the classroom, but because they often lack knowledge about these areas, they can feel overwhelmed. This leads them to revert to more traditional teaching, knowing that it doesn't seem to work either, yet unsure of how to proceed. Understanding that there are vast bodies of research in these areas, these Jonas columns narrowed the focus to emphasize that good teaching practices is often the most effective way to deal with differences. In talking about learning styles, Jonas gives some suggestions on uses multiple methodologies, often simultaneously, to appeal to as many learning styles as possible. The column on learning disabilities helps faculty understand that accommodations to help LD students are really accommodations to help all students and is just good teaching practice. In talking about stereotyping in the classroom, Jonas advocates checking assumptions before teachers react and heightening their awareness of students as both individuals and part of a larger group. Using proven discussion techniques helps faculty facilitate a productive class discussion around differences. And in our column on dealing with knowledge base differences, Jonas suggests resources inside the classroom that the teacher can use that will help all students, and resources outside the classroom that share the learning burden among faculty, students, and staff.

Because of the complexity of this area and because these columns have just scratched the surface on these issues, we have listed some favorite resources at the end of this chapter. The more we educate ourselves about differences, the more we will strive to find ways to address them in the classroom to increase learning and minimize frustration.

Further Reading

Books

1.   Bowen, W., and Bok, D. (1998), *The Shape of the River: Long-term Consequences of Considering Race in College and University Admissions.* New Jersey: Princeton University Press.

2.   Bransford, J., Brown, A., and Cocking, R. (1999). *How People Learn: Brain, Mind, Experience and School.* Washington, D.C.: National Academy Press.

3. Donald, J. (2002), *Learning to Think: Disciplinary Perspectives*. San Franciso: Jossey-Bass.

4. Gardner, H. (1983). *Frames of Mind*. New York: Basic Books Inc.

5. Gardner, H. (1991) *The unschooled mind: how children think and how schools should teach*. New York: Basic Books Inc.

6. Kolb. D. A. and Fry, R. (1975) 'Toward an applied theory of experiential learning; in C. Cooper (ed.) Theories of Group Process, London: John Wiley.

Articles

1. Dunn, R. (2000). *Learning styles: Theory, research, and practice*. National Forum of Applied Educational Research Journal, 13, (1), 3-22.

2. Gardner, H., & Hatch, T. (1989). *Multiple intelligences go to school: Educational implications of the theory of multiple intelligences*. Educational Researcher, 18(8), 4-9.

3. Rudenstine, Neil L.(Autumn, 2001). *The Proper Consideration of Race in Higher Education*. Journal of Blacks in Higher Education; n33 p114-17.

4. Vogel, Susan A.; Leyser, Yona; Wyland, Sharon; Brulle, Andrew. (Summer, 1999), *Students with Learning Disabilities in Higher Education: Faculty Attitude and Practices*. Learning Disabilities Research and Practice; v14 n3 p173-86

Websites

1. LdonLine: The leading web site on learning disabilities for parents, teachers and other professionals.
http://www.ldonline.org

2.   Lubin, J. (2003) University/Education Disability Resources
      http://www.makoa.org/education.htm

3.   Fleming, N. (2001) VARK: A Guide to Learning Styles.
      http://www.vark-learn.com

4.   Diversity Database: Moving Towards Diversity. University
      of Maryland
      http://www.inform.umd.edu/EdRes/topic/Diversity

ACCIDENTAL STEREOTYPING

Dear **Jonas:**

Recently in one of my classes, in which most of the students are men, one of the men used an expression that I felt was inappropriate in mixed company. I responded by saying to this student "You know, Jim, there are women present!"

After the class, one of the women students came and told me that my statement embarrassed her. Then another time, I was talking about a design issue that had to do with aesthetics, and I said to one of the women, "Janice, you're a woman, how does that approach seem to you?" She looked startled at my question, and then simply rolled her eyes. Here I thought I was being sensitive to the women, and my methods ended up backfiring. Where do I go from here?

Searching for the Right Approach

Dear **Searching:**

Historically, many engineering and science classes have been comprised mainly of men. I appreciate the fact that you want the women in your course to feel comfortable and welcome, and that the last thing you want to do is increase the level of unease. As faculty, we should be aware of how our interactions with students are perceived by them, including those from under-represented groups.

Some of us may worry about our ability to treat all students equally and appropriately. We all know that the same words spoken by different instructors can yield very different interpretations. Body language and relationships established with the class and individuals in it play a significant part in communication.

In the first case you described, it really doesn't matter whether the class is a mix of male and female, or what gender the student is who made the comment. If a comment was inappropriate, then that should have been the response: the student's comment was simply inappropriate in a classroom where it's assumed we have a mutual respect for one another. Your response implied that the remark might have been okay if there had been only men in the class.

As for the second situation you described, the general goal should be to treat students in a welcoming and respectful fashion manner that does not cast them as ambassadors or spokespersons for a group (e.g., ethnic or gender group). This is probably what occurred when you asked Janice about the aesthetics question, where you asked her to speak on behalf of all women and report on some assumed consensus viewpoint. In a similar way, it would not be a good approach to ask an African-American student "How does the black community feel about this, Paul?" We already know that students will respond based on their contexts, backgrounds and ranges of experiences.

Something to keep in mind is that many students who are underrepresented in their classes may have been in the majority at their high schools or in a group that was at least 50% of the student body. This is probably true of most women in engineering and science; women make up about half of the high school classes, and only a quarter or less of the classes at most universities. Many students have doubts about whether they belong in their major, particularly if they get a bad grade early on. These self-doubts can be magnified for students in underrepresented groups when they are focused on for their differences.

Another guideline for our interactions with under represented groups is to avoid stereotyping such things as learning styles or abilities. For example, one shouldn't assume that all white males are good at mechanical things, or relate to sports analogies. Going back to your interaction with Janice, you assumed that as a woman, she would take a special interest in the aesthetic part of a design merely because she is female.

All students, regardless of their background, ethnicity, race, etc. have individual strengths and weaknesses that one can learn only by interactions over time. If one approaches students as individuals and at the same time provides a classroom environment that is respectful and open, students will feel free to give their opinions and ideas that will be shaped by their respective experiences as well as cultural backgrounds.

Good luck,

Jonas

Quick Tip: When it comes to interacting with a diverse student population, there really is no quick tip that will apply in all situations. Jonas found this out as he struggled to write a response to this questioner. An excellent resource for diversity issues in higher education can be found at the University of Maryland website: www.inform.umd.edu/Diversity/

APPEALING TO DIFFERENT LEARNING STYLES

Dear **Jonas:**

Last week I was solving a problem with the class at the board. Every time I would do the math, a particular student would raise his hand and asked me what I did. I would do it again, ask him if it was clear and he kept saying "no, can you tell me what you did." Finally I showed him a third time and he just looked exasperated and looked down at his paper. After class, he told me that symbols and visuals were confusing to him and he couldn't learn that way. What is he talking about?

How do I do math without using visuals? Should I suggest he become a drama major?

3.14156 * R^2

Dear **Pi**,

What this student is referring to are differences in how people learn or what are referred to as "learning styles." A person's learning style refers to his/her preferred way of receiving, processing, storing, retrieving, and expressing information. It may also refer to the rate of learning, social conditions needed to learn, or incentives that motivate. Note that the preferred learning style was not the result of any conscious decision but rather a result of his personal evolution. In the case that you described, the language of your interchange with the student is very revealing. He kept saying, "tell me," you kept saying that you "showed him." He was asking for an auditory cue and you were giving him visual information.

Most individuals have a preference for how they learn, and this preference is stronger in some than in others. While there are too many learning style inventories to talk about in depth, let's think about learners as having an auditory (hearing), visual (seeing) or tactile kinesthetic (doing) style. For example, I am an auditory learner and had the same problem as your student when I took an art history class. How could you possibly learn about pictures without being visual?

That was my dilemma. But then a very wise mentor showed me how to use verbal cues to remember visual images. For example, on seeing a picture I would say out loud and write down simultaneously "ah, that's Gainesborough's Blue Boy - he has a blue hat with a white feather in his hand." The verbalization and writing helped me recall the visual.

Your student is asking for the same type of help. While every faculty member cannot (and should not) appeal to every learning style, there are some teaching methods that are easy to integrate into your lessons and quite effective at appealing to many different styles. For example:

- When asking a question in class, we often call on the first or second student to raise a hand. This definitely appeals to the "quick thinker" but what about reflective learners, the students who need to think a minute before formulating an answer? They could get lost. It's a good idea to occasionally ask a question, then tell the class to take a minute to jot down the answer. This gives the reflective/visual person a chance to write and "see", and it allows the quick thinker to formulate a more complete answer. And you've only spent an additional 30 seconds.

- We often present information primarily through an auditory mode, but it's quite easy to make notes available on a Blackboard website, to give a handout on particularly complicated material, or use an overhead with visual images once in a while. This will appeal to both auditory AND visual learners. Try to build in something "to do" for the tactile/kinesthetic learner. Again something as simple as having students write in class, or draw a picture. I once asked a class to write the definition of three terms, then draw a diagram showing the connection between the terms. Some students had outstanding definitions, some outstanding diagrams - all of them understood the concept better.

Students entering college now have experienced more visual and active learning in secondary schools, so they may need help adapting to the primarily auditory style of many college courses. Some basic points to think about:

1. There are NO right or wrong styles - just different styles.

2. We all tend to have a preference, but not an exclusionary style.

3. We all vary our preference over time and based on the task (e.g., I couldn't possibly have learned to use a computer from a book).

4. Course content may favor certain learning styles (e.g., art history favoring visual learners), but the instructor should keep other styles in mind during lesson preparation.

5. Effective learners are able to ADAPT to different styles and effective teachers assist them in doing this.

It is a question of style, but using good teaching methods in general is the best way to appeal to everyone.

Jonas

Quick Tip: For a more detailed description of visual, auditory, and tactile/kinesthetic learners, see the Illinois Online Network's "Learning Styles and the Online Environment" page, available at: www.ion.illinois.edu/IONresources/instructionalDesign/learningStyles.html

---

Richard Felder offers another perspective on learning styles on his web site, "Resources in Science and Engineering Education." His "Index of Learning Styles" page www.ncsu.edu/felder-public/ILSpage.html) offers descriptions of learning preferences based on four dimensions — active/reflective, sensing/intuitive, visual/verbal, and sequential/global. This page includes links to a learning styles inventory, which can be used by students to assess their preferences, and suggestions for how students can help themselves when they encounter teaching styles that do not match their preferred learning style.

MULTIMEDIA

Dear Jonas,

I read your column on learning styles, and it sounds like an awful lot of work to develop different styles of presentation for different students. Is there anything I can do to make this easier?

Out of Style

Dear **Out of Style**,

Using multimedia materials is one way to provide information that meets the needs of a variety of learners. By its very definition, "multimedia" presents information in a way that provides more than one type of input, combining visual presentations with audio or interactive elements, therefore appealing to multiple learning styles.

Examples of multimedia materials may include any of the following:

- Video clips - these can appeal to both visual and auditory learners.
- Interactive illustrations of ideas present information visually and allow students to interact with the content - this is appealing to active or kinesthetic learners.
- Case studies or application problems that place concepts in a context are beneficial to global thinkers.
- Tutorials and practice quizzes - these activities may appeal to those who need extra time for reflection.

Many of these materials can be used either for in-class presentations or as supplementary materials for students. Creating these materials can be costly and time-consuming, but there are many sources of existing multimedia elements that you may find useful.

First, check to see what your textbook publisher provides. Many publishers now provide web sites with multimedia that supports a text at no cost. Some package these materials as a "cartridge" that can be easily loaded into the Blackboard course management system.

You can also check with your colleagues who have taught this course or similar courses recently. You might find that some of them have compiled nice collections of multimedia links and files that they could share with you. Another source of multimedia is Merlot (www.merlot.org), an online, searchable repository of media elements created for higher education. The Merlot web site is a free and open resource that is searchable by discipline area and through keywords. Each entry provides a link to the actual location of the material (typically at another university). Many entries are peer reviewed and include sample assignments that explain how to use the material. Use of some materials requires a nominal fee and/or copyright notice, but many can be linked to freely.

Finally, there are many commercial multimedia products available that you may find valuable. Recently I mentioned using a web-based homework system. In addition to providing individualized instruction and feedback, some of these products present content through interactive media that provides benefits to a wide range of students.

Jonas

Quick Tip: You do not need to immediately add all of these elements to every course that you teach. Try adding one or two aspects of multimedia, as appropriate to the material. Multimedia usage entails presentation of information to affect more than one form of learning style - a visual element may be effective for illustrating science applications, while a tutorial may be effective for beginner pro-

---

> gramming. Once you get started, you may find more and more opportunities and materials that facilitate different learning styles.

LEARNING DISABILITIES

Dear **Jonas:**

I'm very puzzled by one of my students. He's always in class, always on time, asks questions in class, raises his hand to answer questions, and turns in homework on time. In general, he is trying hard but is failing all the exams and quizzes. When I asked him to come to my office to talk about his progress, he finally told me that he has a learning disability. He had access to a lot of services in high school and says that he did very well, got mostly A's and B's. He never thought college would be this hard. I'm really torn as to what to do. While I admire his diligence and hard work, he's just not passing. Can you help me?

Conflicted Instructor

Dear **C. I.,**

Good for you for noticing that output didn't match input and talking directly to the student. There are many issues in this question, so let me try to address each area. First, this is not an unusual scenario for learning disabled students new to college. Many students who have a learning disability (LD) feel labeled or stigmatized from high school experiences and often want to begin with a "clean slate" in college. Unfortunately, that can often mean not telling anyone about their LD. So your first suggestion may be to ask him if he has been to the Disabilities Resource Center. If not, try to encourage him to seek out services to support his learning, especially during this crucial transition year. Some students may need out-of-class accommodations such as extra time for exams; others may need help with note taking, which the DRC can arrange.

Your second concern seems to be what you can do as an instructor. First, remember that learning disabled students have been accepted to college because they have the intellectual ability to succeed; in fact LD students often have very high IQs. Their difficulty is in processing information, not intellectual capability. For example, think how difficult it would be for you to teach a class in English if all your students asked you questions in French and you didn't know French. In many ways, this type of cognitive disconnection is what LD students experience. There are many things you can do as an instructor to support the learning of LD students. In fact, research has shown that strategies teachers use to help LD students actually help ALL students. Most of the strategies I'll suggest are good teaching practices that involve helping students understand HOW to learn more effectively in college.

In general, experts on learning disabilities advise:
- Use the board - write objectives, assignments and outlines of the class on the board to assist students with organizational difficulties
- Show and Tell - provide multiple models, examples, and illustrations of new concepts. Ask students to create additional problems for each other and the class using the concepts.
- Teach note taking - in courses that require note taking, teach students how to take notes in a series of steps. In the beginning provide a detailed outline, reduce the amount of detail as the quarter continues until students are demonstrating they can generate their own.
- Use memory devices - try to develop mnemonic techniques to help students remember complex concepts, then have them develop their own mnemonics for subsequent complex concepts.

- Give frequent feedback - break material down into smaller chunks and give students frequent feedback either graded or ungraded; try using classroom assessment techniques such as a "one minute" paper and so forth.
- Utilize technology - technology provides opportunities for students who need strong visual and/or tactile approaches to learning
- Use alternative assessments - offer alternative activities for students when possible: a comprehensive project versus a final exam; an occasional group activity rather than all individual work

For those who primarily lecture:
- Make it interactive - add two minute breaks at appropriate junctions and ask students to summarize the lecture so far, or come up with questions about the material, or compare points with a partner. All of these activities allow students time to process, reflect, and apply what you've talked about so far.
- Add visuals to lectures - this incorporates the visual senses and provides advanced organizers for students with organizational processing difficulties. You can write on the board, use power point or even an old fashion overhead.
- Give verbal lecture cues - use verbal statements to let student know this is important. For example, "this is important to remember;" "there are three areas to remember"
- Remember to PAUSE - Pausing cues students that what you've said is important, it also provides a few seconds for students to catch up

In general, helping LD students involves being an effective, caring teacher who tunes in to the needs of the class and provides a variety of ways for students to process information.

This student knew he was LD. Sometimes when you notice this kind of behavior, a student may have mild learning disabilities that went undiagnosed in high school because the student was smart enough to compensate. If you suspect that a student may have an undiagnosed learning disability, you might suggest they talk to someone in the Disabilities Resource Center.

If you provide an environment that is comfortable so students can approach you when their learning strategies fail, is flexible and provides alternatives, and gives frequent feedback so that students can make adjustments, you'll be providing an environment that supports ALL students.

Good Luck,

Jonas

Quick Tip: Students are not required to inform faculty if they have disabilities. However, they are encouraged to do so early in the term, so appropriate accommodations can be made. Our Disabilities Resource Center suggests that all faculty include a statement on their syllabus that reads something like:

I encourage students with disabilities, including "invisible" disabilities like chronic diseases or learning disabilities, to meet with me Individually (within the first week of classes) and discuss appropriate accommodations which might be helpful for you. Your disability must be verifiable; on campus the Disability Resource Center can provide you with information and other assistance.

ON ISSUES OF DIVERSITY

Dear **Jonas,**

I know that the University has put a lot of energy into recruiting historically underrepresented students and helping them succeed. But when I look out on my class, I still see very few students of color. While I don't have any influence on the recruiting process, is there anything I can do as an instructor to help these students stay in a science or math based major? Is there something we're doing as instructors that keeps minority students from wanting to be science, math or engineering majors? What can we, as faculty, do to diversify our SMET student population?

Cogitating with a Conscience

Dear **Cogitating,**

Like many "Jonas" column topics, this one has had innumerable books, articles, and theses written about it. For the purpose of this column, I will touch on a couple of facets of this complex issue. Fortunately, I recently attended a lecture by Karl Reid from MIT's program on minorities in engineering. Below are some important points that he made about some issues related to diversity in our engineering student body. Keep in mind, as I always caution, that we should look at each student as an individual with his or her own set of strengths and weaknesses.

First, Karl pointed out that we need to recognize a number of external factors that conspire against anyone succeeding in this field, especially students of color coming from urban settings. These include limited access to decent housing and healthcare, increased levels of crime, and discrimination on a number of levels. Their K-12 educational experience may include fewer AP course offerings, contain disruptive urban learning environments, and uncertified math/science teachers.

Students who overcome these challenges often enter the university with an inflated view of their ability; this often leads to a "crash," when grades received do not reflect their own perceptions of their ability. Further, it has been documented that faculty often have low expectations of these students and that a so-called "null" environment may exist. This is a void created when a minority student does not have a relationship with faculty or staff within this new engineering environment. This creates a perception on the part of the student that he or she is not really welcome or wanted, and this lack of encouragement is equated with discouragement. This point is particularly important for instructors, because when compared to white students, minority students are three times as likely to rate teachers as important factors in their success. If these students do not receive signals from their teachers that they are capable of achieving success in their classes, it may instigate this "null" environment, even if done unknowingly. In addition, the financial strains imposed by college costs tend to weigh more heavily on minority students, and they may also tend to have less of a sense of "belongingness" to the university, which in turn is connected to a lower level of student involvement.

Despite all of these challenges, the number of engineering degrees earned by African-American, Latino and Asian/Pacific Island students has increased fairly significantly during the 1990's. However in 2000, only 5% of science and engineering graduates were black and 4.1% were Hispanic. So how do we, as instructors, ensure that we're not setting up further impediments to minority student success? How do we make sure we're not partners in creation of a "null" environment?

Karl described the development in these students of something called "self-efficacy" - the student's sense that they can exercise control over their own success. The student's sense of self-efficacy determines whether the success (or failure) is attributable to his or her abilities or simply to luck. This characteristic is more than self-confidence: it is about self-identity (seeing someone like themselves in the roles that they are preparing for), meeting reasonable but challenging expectations, having a high degree of integrity and accountability, making good choices, and acquiring good academic skills and practices. Faculty usually assume that most of our students arrive at the university with some core of self-efficacy that we can shape and enhance during their college careers. Minority students may arrive with less of a foundation, and it has to be constructed in fairly short order.

One way to build student self-efficacy is through special residence hall programs and freshman seminar programs that focus on the elements described above. In the classroom, instructors can contribute to this building process in their courses by considering the following points:

- Maintain high, but reasonable, expectations of minority students' abilities. Initiate pre-assessment activities to understand the knowledge and skill that students bring to your class.

- For group work, assign minority students to groups with mixed abilities and mixed racial composition. Seeking outside help can sometimes be viewed as a sign of weakness due to the inner city social construct, so have a set of guidelines and procedures to help students understand the value of group work.

- To avoid the "null" environment, always be clear about learning objectives and the grading/reward system, and recognize learning successes among all students. This will benefit all students, regardless of race.

- Give regular attributional feedback. If the student's self-perceived ability is high, then success is attributed to ability and the effort put forward. However, if the student's self perceived ability is low then success is attributed to luck! Provision of clear, specific feedback to students on the knowledge and skill they possess that led to their success will help them see that it is more than luck.

- Set challenging goals for the students, but match this with a high level of support through special office hours, organized study groups and tutoring.

- Leverage intrinsic cultural constructs. In the classroom, you may want to utilize multiple measures of assessment that include oral as well as written, as many students come from a strong oral tradition. Outside the classroom, utilize the group dynamic of fellow minority students/organizations. While this may seem like a contradiction of the point made previously about mixing groups, it represents the tightrope that we need to walk between bringing these students into the mainstream while still promoting their cultural identity.

- Challenge racial and gender stereotypes by promoting female and minority engineers as role models. These engineers can be introduced in the class through guest lecturers, field trips, readings and other assignments that promote diversity.

As I've noted above, by implementing some of these approaches in our classroom environment, we'll actually benefit all of our students, each of whom needs some degree of self-efficacy development. All students need to see the same diversity that exists in the world outside the university. And, as Karl has proven in his work at MIT, these approaches will particularly benefit those students whose backgrounds have led to a lower sense of self-efficacy. If we desire a more diverse student body, instructors need to, and can be, important partners in this process.

Thanks for your question and good luck.

Jonas

Quick Tip: An important part of Karl's talk dealt with so-called "attribution theory," which describes the relationship between a student's perceived ability, actual performance, and the reasons they assign for their success or failure. The following matrix relates these three issues. For example, when a student's perceived ability is low and they are successful in what they do (e.g., they receive an A in a course), they attribute it to luck.

Matrix of Attribution Theory
To What Do Students Attribute Their Performance?
(Karl Reid, MIT, 2003)

		Perceived Ability	
		High	**Low**
Performance	**Success**	Ability/Effort	Luck
	Failure	(Lack of) Effort	(Lack of) Ability

Chapter 8
Dear Jonas:

When is an "A" an "A"?

Jacqueline Isaacs

As students, we have all experienced the anxiety of waiting for final grades. We wondered when the grades would be computed, and when would they be posted. We were embarrassed if we saw the professor in the hallway, because we were sure s/he remembered the stupid mistake that we made on question 2. We looked at the professor as an all-powerful being that could make or break our academic grade point average. But now we are on the other side…

When we see our students on campus after an exam, do we recall their mistakes? Did we actually grade their exam or did a graduate teaching assistant grade it? Or perhaps we cringe because we have not even begun to grade the exams. While faculty may enjoy teaching and find it rewarding in many ways, they rarely enjoy grading.

When new faculty first begin teaching undergraduate classes, they may not have given thought to how they plan to assess student work. Perhaps they graded student homework assignments as a graduate teaching assistant. Their own experience as students reminds them that they could select among different grading schemes. The most common options include absolute grading standards, normative grading standards – where a class curve is developed, or variations on scaling grades. Faculty also may not have received guidance on designing appropriate homework, exams, projects or other assignments. This skill is particularly important since grad-

---

ing a poorly designed exam can require significant extra time.

Before determining the suitability of a grading scheme, it is important to consider the purpose of grades (Walvoord and Anderson, 1998). While some faculty may view grading as an instrument to "weed out" the strong students from the weak, others may regard grading as an opportunity to assess whether all students have mastered a particular skill level necessary for the next course in the sequence. No matter what grading approach is preferred, there is agreement that grades should provide information on a student's level of knowledge (Erickson and Strommer, 1991).

The apprehension that some students have with respect to their grades can sometimes lead to barriers for their learning (Davis, 1993). If faculty are aware of student anxieties, then they can take proactive approaches to reduce the barriers, by working towards changing student perceptions. Instead of endorsing the faculty role as that of an evaluator who looks for the limitations in student abilities (which can be threatening), faculty can present themselves as supportive coaches, who work to prepare students to meet clearly defined challenges. Communication throughout the course can ease student anxieties. At the beginning of the term, faculty can define their expectations for graded assignments and their grading policies (Wankat and Oreovicz, 1993 and Davidson and Ambrose, 1994). Since most students want to know how their scores compare with the rest of the class after exams, faculty should communicate the average test scores, and their interpretation of the associated letter grade. Positive reinforcement and encouragement to students who have received low scores will often offer more incentives to students than the threat of failure (Milton et al, 1986).

Through their college experiences, undergraduates will hopefully have learned important lessons regarding responsibility and evaluation by the time they matriculate. Faculty have an obligation to teach students two things that will help them succeed as adults: to take responsibility for themselves, and to carefully choose how to prioritize their time (Lowman, 1995).

In this chapter, Jonas addresses issues of fairness in testing techniques and how to handle uncomfortable situations where students perceive others have an unfair advantage. Jonas also looks at process issues such as the impact of late grades on students, and assigning letter versus numerical grades. Test taking anxiety can also takes it toll on student performance, and Jonas shares techniques to help students who suffer from undo anxiety. Lastly our system of grading can sometimes seem incomprehensible to students, Jonas helps a reader understand the student perspective and anxiety around grades.

Further Reading

Books

1. Davidson, Cliff I. and Susan A. Ambrose (1994), *The New Professor's Handbook: A Guide to Teaching and Research in Engineering and Science*, Anker Publishing Company, Inc., Bolton, MA.

2. Davis, Barbara Gross (1993), *Tools for Teaching*. San Francisco, CA: Jossey-Bass Publishers.

3. Erickson, Bette LaSere and Diane Weltner Strommer (1991), *Teaching College Freshmen*. San Francisco, CA: Jossey-Bass Publishers.

4. Lowman, Joseph (1995), *Mastering the Techniques of Teaching*. San Francisco, CA: Jossey-Bass Publishers.

5.   Milton, Ohmer, Howard R. Pollio and James A. Eison (1986), *Making Sense of College Grades*. San Francisco, CA: Jossey-Bass Publishers.

6.   Walvoord, Barbara E and Virginia Johnson Anderson (1998), *Effective Grading: A Tool for Learning and Assessment*. San Francisco, CA: Jossey-Bass Publishers.

7.   Wankat, Phillip C. and Frank S. Oreovicz (1993), *Teaching Engineering*. New York, NY: McGraw-Hill.

Websites

1.   University of Washington, Office of Educational Assessment, Faculty Resource on Grading (FROG) http://depts.washington.edu/grading/grading.htm
2.   Carnegie Mellon University, Eberly Center for Teaching Excellence, http://www.cmu.edu/eberlycenter/index.html

WHY WE TEST

Dear **Jonas,**

Yesterday, I had the following conversation with one of my colleagues:

Me: Hi Bill. Sorry that I missed the meeting this morning. I gave a midterm exam yesterday, and they are taking forever to grade.

Colleague: Why don't you give short answer tests? Or just give multiple-choice tests with bubble answer sheets; then a computer could grade it.

Me: I've thought about that. I know that it would save me tons of time, but the partial-credit tests let me better see the extent of the students' comprehension, and many of the students really hate multiple-choice tests.

Colleague: But then the grading takes time away from your other activities - like the meeting that you missed this morning - and, more importantly, since you're tenure-track, you should be spending your time doing research, not grading.

This conversation led me to think about how much time and effort we, and the students, put into the whole testing process. We have to prepare the tests, review for the tests, take time to give the tests, record grades, hand the graded tests back and go over them, and then respond to students' complaints about the grading. Of course, the students themselves have to spend a lot of time preparing for and taking tests.

My question is: wouldn't it be a lot easier for faculty, and wouldn't more learning be accomplished by the students, if we simply didn't test at all? What is the real point of giving tests?

Tired of Testing

Dear **ToT,**

Tests are a method by which we try to evaluate students' understanding of or ability to apply the material from a course; to answer questions or to solve problems - sometimes the questions are like ones they've seen before, and sometimes they are asked to use the basic principles and apply them in new, creative ways.

Such evaluations, even though imperfect, are important for three distinct groups: the students, the instructors, and external parties who hire our students or consider them for things like graduate school. Moreover, for both the student and the instructor, tests are an important learning device.

For the students, studying for tests is an important part of the learning process. It creates the need for the students to review material, to go over a wide variety of questions/problems, to isolate the most important and most basic principles, and to ask questions about fine points. The returned graded test provides a way for students to evaluate which topics they have learned and which topics need more attention. Also, studying hard and then getting a high grade is a great feeling, which can be very motivating for students.

For instructors, tests are one common method for assigning letter grades which are supposed to be indicative of a student's mastery of the course material; we are required to produce these letter grades. However, instructors should also learn from tests.

Coming up with test questions which accurately reflect learning objectives for the course really forces an instructor to think about the topics which are the most fundamental in his/her course. The grades on the tests should help the instructor realize which objectives he/she needs to give more time to, or if all of the subject matter has been covered adequately. An individual student's grade lets the instructor know whether that student needs extra work on specific areas. Finally, giving a student extra help and then seeing their grade go way up is rewarding and very motivating for the instructor!

In the end, the letter grades that we assign end up on a student's transcript, which is important for the student to graduate and to then continue working in industry or working on an advanced degree. Despite the fact that everyone knows that there are limitations to what can be measured by written tests, they are the most common mechanism used for assigning grades. For many employers and academic institutions, a student's grades are one important device to evaluate competence. This means that even after a student's graduation, the tests that you give, and the grades that the student receives on them, can affect the student's life far down the road.

Testing and grading are time-consuming and painful in many ways, but, for all the reasons given above, it is important to pay serious attention to the evaluation and encouragement of student learning in your courses.

As a final comment, I should mention that, of course, testing is not the only way to measure learning. Projects, presentations, problems, and other instruments can provide the same feedback, incentives, and contribute to grades, as well. In fact, they may create more genuine opportunities for learning. However, the points that I made above apply to these alternate evaluation methods as well. There is simply no way around it: evaluations of learning are important for many reasons, and any well-designed measure of learning will take significant time and effort from both the students and the faculty.

Jonas

Quick Tip: Read upcoming Chalk Talk columns for suggestions on what types of tests to give, and for some alternative methods of summative evaluation other than the traditional exams and papers.

HELPING STUDENTS PREPARE FOR AND TAKE EXAMS

Dear **Jonas,**

With final exams approaching, my students are asking my advice on how to prepare for the exam. Somehow telling them to study hard and solve lots of problems doesn't seem to be enough, but that's what I did when I was a student. Any advice?

Feeling Inadequate

Dear **Feeling,**

At its core your advice is sensible since most exams in math, science and engineering are problem-solving activities. Unfortunately, preparation for some students, especially freshmen, entails simply reviewing solutions to problems done in class, in the book or for homework and understanding with the solutions. Other students might actually re-work the problems.

My last column talked about approaches to help our students learn problem-solving skills/strategies. So, when I get questions from students about exam preparation, I suggest that they approach preparation for exams strategically as well. To facilitate this, I first ask them to describe the difference between taking an exam and doing a homework problem. Typical responses include remarks such as:

- I won't have my book or notes to refer to.
- There's not enough time to use the book anyhow.
- I can't ask my friends.
- Homework problems are on the subject we just studied. I don't have to identify what type of problem it is as I do on an exam.

- I have lots of time to do my homework but only two hours for the final exam.

In response, I suggest that a good strategy might be to replicate exam conditions as the final stage of preparation. After individually reviewing the subject material and preparing, I suggest to students that they engage in study groups in the following manner:

1. Students should borrow or purchase a book of solved problems in the subject from the bookstore. Schaum's Outlines and many others publish them in a wide range of subjects (literally compilations of hundreds of solved problems in physics, math chemistry, etc.) Splitting the cost among four or five study group members keeps the cost manageable. They could also use previously unsolved problems from the textbook, but generally, entire solution sets are not included in texts.
2. In turn, each group member selects a problem and gives it to the group. Time available is an issue in exams, so an alarm clock is set for 10 minutes or so, and all try to solve the problem independently. If you wanted to give them an old exam, you could urge them to use it in the same way. The time constraint does add a degree of stress that will exist at exam time.
3. If the exam will be closed-book, then students shouldn't use books when solving problems. If it's an open-book exam, then students should index the key pages and practice identifying and applying appropriate formulas/operations.
4. At the end of the time period, students can compare solutions with others and with the solution in the book. If anyone had difficulty with classification or concept application, a discussion should ensue. An understanding of any mistakes in problem solving usually leads to a

richer understanding of the material. I often tell my students that one way to know if you have learned something is to teach it to someone having difficulty.

5. Students can repeat the process until all subjects have been reviewed extensively. The learning objectives stated on the course syllabus should provide guidance here.

In my experience, another situation that causes trouble for students is poor time management during the exam. We've all had students tell us that they spent too much time on the first problem and had to rush the rest of the way. To help students with time management issues, I offer the following suggestions (guidelines, not hard and fast rules) to my students just before handing out the exam:

1. Read all problems before writing anything. Jot notes for yourself next to problems regarding relevant equations and definitions. This will help when you return to those problems, and show you know the information if you run out of time before completing them.

2. Note the point value of problems to decide where to spend more time.

3. Attack the problem you find easiest first. It may not be problem #1.

4. Be aware of time passing. If there are eight problems on a 120-minute exam (that's an average of 15 minutes per problem), spend no more than 15 minutes on the first problem tackled before consciously deciding whether to continue or move on to another.

5. After completing each problem, reassess the time remaining. (If the first problem was done in 9 minutes you now have more than 17 minutes per problem remaining.)

6. If you have time left, use the last minutes to double-check your calculations.

I hope you find some of these suggestions on student strategies for preparation and for taking exams to be useful. Good luck.

Jonas

Quick Tip: Even if students don't ask about preparing for exams, you could spark a discussion by asking them about the difference between solving a homework problem and solving a problem on an exam. You could also talk briefly about the six points on exam taking "prior" to exam day, since students are more likely to "hear" you under less stressful conditions. Finally, you might consider offering a verbal and/or written time check through the duration of the exam to keep students on track.

ANSWERING QUESTIONS DURING EXAMS

Dear **Jonas:**

I gave an exam last week in my sophomore class, which had 75 students. I had done the problems myself and used the rule of three for the students to determine a 60-minute duration. There were no typos on the exam. The only difference between the exam, and the homework problems (to which the students had been given solutions), is that the exam asked questions/problems that they had not seen before. That is, students were asked to apply what they had learned to a new situation. I cannot be-LIEVE the number of questions I received during the exam. "Professor, does this answer look right to you?" "Professor is this how you solve this question?" "Professor, is this a '2'?" Out of the fifty or so questions that I answered (I'm not kidding), about 85% of the

---

time, the students were looking for some sort of "reassurance" from me. Granted, I have been very approachable throughout the term, and I have told them to think of me as their coach, but sheeez! This is ridiculous. So I ask: Am I doing something wrong? Are these students particularly needy or has this "freshman year handholding" gone too far?

Fairly Frustrated

Dear **Frustrated,**

First of all, you're not doing anything wrong, you're actually doing a lot of things right! Making sure that the test can be finished in the allotted time, proofreading for typos, and using application questions/problems are all techniques that help ensure that the exam will be fair yet challenging. That said however, remember that test situations often generate anxiety, even in the most confident students. Think of our own situations as teachers. Even if we've been teaching for 30 years and won numerous awards, as soon as a colleague asks to come in and observe the class, many of us get anxious and nervous - it's only human. The same holds true for students, especially when a major portion of their final grade is based on a "high stakes" exam. They may also have had experiences where previous professors answered or even encouraged questions during the exam so they may feel this is perfectly appropriate to do.

Frequent questioning during the exam can be annoying, not only to you as the instructor, but to other students who might loose their concentration when someone asks a question or you clarify a point to everyone. So to help minimize the number of questions, here are a few suggestions. You might ask a colleague or graduate student to read over your exam first to see whether any questions should be clarified. Sometimes what seems perfectly clear to the writer isn't so clear to the test taker. At the beginning of the exam, you could tell students to look over the test immediately and ask about any ambiguities like "is this a 2" up front. This not only gives them an opportunity to ask their questions, but also models a good test taking technique: to read over the entire exam first and to formulate a strategy for solving the entire exam. Make clear your expectations during the exam. For example if you do not want to give feedback on a problem solving approach ("is this how I do this problem"), then tell them that. If you will answer questions, but only when they come up to your desk quietly so as not to disturb others, then tell them that as well. You may also decide to make exams only one of many ways (papers, projects, etc.) by which students can demonstrate their knowledge and get feedback on their progress; this takes some of the "high stakes" aspect out of the test and lowers student anxiety.

Students, especially freshmen and sophomores, may struggle with application-type questions/problems, especially if applications have not been a significant part of illustrations or homework. Many times their knowledge is based on memorizing rather than understanding, so if you deviate from the formula they get confused and nervous. Application is a higher level skill than comprehension (from Bloom's Taxonomy*) and requires higher level thinking. Prepare them for this transition. Homework can include application of a concept that they just learned, or you can even ask them to generate application problems as a homework assignment.

We may never completely prevent students from asking questions during an exam, and probably shouldn't, but by carefully preparing the exam and our expectations during exams, we will help minimize the number.

Jonas

Quick Tip: Try having students generate possible application test questions as a homework assign-

---

ment and then use a number of their questions on your exam or on a practice exam given to them in advance. This technique will help them learn the material in a more thorough manner.

*Learning is hierarchically categorized from a) knowledge to b) comprehension to c) application to d) analysis to e) synthesis to f) evaluation. See resources below for more information.

1   Bloom, B. (1956). Taxonomy of Educational Objectives: Cognitive Domain. New York, NY: David McKay.

2.   Overview of Bloom's Taxonomy with additional links http://faculty.washington.edu/krumme/guides/bloom.html

MULTIPLE CHOICE TESTING

Dear **Jonas,**

I teach a couple of large introductory sections and use multiple-choice exams. Some of my colleagues say that is "smart teaching" and others say it's "lazy teaching". What do you think? Are there ways to increase the effectiveness of using multiple-choice tests?

A) **Smart**
B) **Lazy**

Dear **A and/or B,**

I say "yes" to both sides depending on HOW and WHY instructors use multiple-choice tests. Multiple choice testing is an efficient way to get feedback on learning from large sections and I'll talk about several good reasons to use them. Effective multiple choice testing is also very difficult to do without a lot of thought and preparation. Actually, a study showed that new instructors needed almost 30 minutes PER question to construct a "good" multiple-choice exam. So there is a balance in time spent on multiple choice versus other forms of testing if you want to do it right. When should you use multiple choice testing? Most experts will tell you that multiple choice test are good when you want to test the breadth of student learning with less depth, as in a survey course. They're also good when you want to test different levels of learning around a concept to see if students have not only understood a concept, but can use it as well. Multiple choice testing also provides some professional development for students, since most of them will have to take some form of high stakes standardized test (licensure, grad school) in their future. Multiple-choice tests can also be effective when it is not necessary for you to determine HOW they formulated their answer only that they CAN formulate the answer.

There are several benefits to using a multiple-choice format. Besides being easy to grade, you can correlate specific questions to specific learning objectives for your course and feedback on areas of your curriculum if a large percentage of students fail a specific question that is well constructed. You can also compare performance from class to class or year to year if you have a large, reliable question bank. Although there are valid educational reasons to use multiple choice testing, remember that construction a meaningful multiple choice test is very difficult and time consuming, so don't wait until the day before the test to decide to use this format.

If you decide that multiple choice testing is the best format to assess the learning in your course, here are some points from the literature to consider as you construct the test items.

1. Is the item clear and concise? Writing good stems (i.e. the question) takes considerable thought. Be sure that you use active voice, avoid common typos, and have all essential information in the stem.

2. Stems can be in the form of questions or incomplete statements. Questions are clearer to understand as opposed to incomplete sentences that are open to interpretation.

3. State questions or statements in the positive form. Using negatives is not a way to not confuse students - Huh?? If you must use negatives, emphasize them somehow in *italics* or **bold** to alert students.

4. Write the correct response immediately after you write the stem and keep it brief and simple.

5. Add distractors (i.e. the wrong answers) AFTER you've written the right answer and be sure that the form of the distracters matches the form of the right answer. Long right answers and short distractors clue students into the answer.

6. Check the grammar in distractors. The wrong tense will alert students that this is a distractor.

7. Don't make the distractors too similar to the correct answer. Your goal should be to determine student learning, comprehension and ability to apply information, not to "trick" the students into choosing the wrong answer. (Remember, they'll be nervous and under time pressure as it is.)

8. Be sure that you test higher levels of learning in your test. It is possible to construct multiple-choice questions that test problem solving, application, and synthesis skills. Our tendency is to keep multiple-choice tests to knowledge and comprehension levels only.

9. Use "none of the above" or "all of the above" with caution (some experts say never), especially with "best answer" stems. However, this format may be helpful in stems that involve mathematical operation. Sometimes, students have been able to successfully argue for the "some" or "all of the above" response, when I had intended for only one to be the correct answer.

10. Make sure the length of the test is appropriate to the time students have to take the test.
11. Check to be sure that you've distributed answers keys (A, B, C, D) evenly and randomly over the exam
12. Lastly and most importantly, have someone else review your test. Ask your reviewer to tell you if there might be multiple interpretations of your stem, if there might be another possible right answer you didn't consider, if your right answer is too obvious or if there are spelling/typo errors.

One of the limitations of multiple-choice tests is the inability to see how students formulate their answers. If you need to understand thought processes for a couple of questions, you can still use the multiple-choice format. For those one or two questions, add a simple addendum to that question - "Explain your choice" and give them a couple of lines to do it. (This will also help you discern which students are good guessers and which have actually mastered the material.)

Remember multiple choice tests should not be designed to trick students, but rather to be rigorous assessment tools of student learning. There is much more information about writing good multiple-choice tests. If you're interested in more depth, try Professor John Sevenair's website at Xavier University (http://webusers.xula.edu/jsevenai/objective/guidelines.html) it's full of tips, research, and examples. There's also a good site at Indiana to check out as well (http://www.indiana.edu/~best/write_better_ tests.shtml).

Jonas

Quick Tip: As an assignment - or for extra credit - you can ask students to formulate possible multiple-choice questions from the course material. This gives them a means to interact with the material, test their own understanding, and anticipate the kind of questions that may actually be asked. It can serve both as a way to enforce that they read assignments, as well as a way to provide a format they can use in studying. It will also give you a bank of possible questions (which you may need to further adapt, refine and polish).

UNFAIR TESTING

Dear **Jonas**,

Yesterday I gave my class a test. At the end of the period only about half the students had finished the exam. The students started getting very vocal, complaining about needing more time, asking whether they could do it over, claiming that the test wasn't fair, and so on. So I told them that for those who didn't finish, I would grade only the part they had completed. After class, the students who had finished the test came to me and were very angry. They said it wasn't fair: since they had finished the test, why should these other students have less work graded? Now I've got everybody in the class mad at me. What should I do?

Tested Out

Dear **Tested Out**,

First, think about what you might have done to avoid this. For example, did you try the test yourself to see how long it took you to do it? Even though you're an expert, you often get a feel for how much time it might actually take if you try to answer your own questions. It's always best to try any assignments yourself beforehand so that you have a better understanding of what's involved in doing the work. If you have a TA or grad student working for you, you could ask him or her to take the test and note how long it took; you can then adjust the questions accordingly. If this happens again, you can try a couple of strategies. You could tell students that you're going to grade the entire test, but because so many students had problems with it, you're willing to drop one grade this quarter (assuming that you are sure your future tests can be done in the allotted time). If you believe in extra credit, you could give students an opportunity to make up points.

With this class, you're already in a bind. It's best to be frank with the group and tell them you were really surprised that they couldn't finish the test in time. You might also consider telling them that those who want the test to count should let you know, and for the others, you'll disregard the test grade in the final grade calculations. You should then set the policy clearly with the class for future tests. They'll appreciate that you've heard their concerns and are planning to address them in the future.

Jonas

Quick Tip: To approximate whether an allotted exam time will be adequate for students, determine the time it takes you to complete the exam and multiply by three.

UNDERSTANDING GRADING PRACTICES

Dear **Jonas**,

I recently gave my first exam and the average was 63. I think the exam was harder than I thought, and one problem may have been confusing. The average is a bit lower than last year, but I understand it's not all that unusual, and I can deal with it through by curving or by scaling the final grade.

After returning the exam, some students were upset. One student was particularly anxious and agitated. She had gotten a 59 on the exam and was deeply concerned that she was failing. She said her parents were going to kill her if she failed. I tried to reassure her that she was not failing, but she just doesn't seem to get the concept of curving. I'm baffled and not quite sure how to respond.

Baffled

Dear **Baffled,**

This type of reaction is not at all uncommon for students who have never encountered curving or scaling. They also might not be clear on how the final course grade is determined. It's not surprising that some students will be quite stressed-out. The reaction and resulting anxiety may be more widespread than you think since many may be scared or embarrassed to approach you and discuss it. Some will simply view the situation as hopeless, might lose motivation and might give up on the course, when with some additional help they might end up passing with flying colors. Other students who are in danger of failing also need to be given additional assistance and pointed in the direction of help resources.

I recommend that you take some time to discuss grades with the whole class. Make it clear how the final grade will be determined. You might explain about year-to-year variations in exam difficulty and other factors. You might give examples of how the final grade is calculated for a student who makes the average grade on the exams, quizzes and homework.

Students want to know how they stand in a course. At the very least, you should announce a realistic cutoff grade on the exam. Make it clear that students with exam grades below the cutoff are in danger of failing the course and must come to speak with you about their options. In fact, since some students are reluctant to visit their instructors outside of class, this is a good time to encourage all other concerned students to speak with you.

When speaking with students one-on-one, you might explore with them the difficulties they're having and help them develop new strategies. Are they strategically problem-solving or just mimicking example solutions? Do they have the background needed for the course? What are the difficult topics? Are they part of a study group? Are they aware of the extra help services? Are they spending enough time on the course? Many students are unaware that two hours outside of class per hour in class is typically needed, but some may need more.

Are they experiencing test anxiety? I tell students that the best way to relieve test anxiety is to be very well pre-pared: do extra problems from the textbook, discuss the difficult problems with me, a tutor, classmates, or a study group.

Finally for additional advice, students should be encouraged to visit their academic advisors. These folks have provided advice or referrals for many students on exam-taking, withdrawals and the curriculum options for students.

Jonas

QuickTip: Consider discussing your grading system with the class before the exams, so students understand your expectations. If you include this information your syllabus, you set clear guidelines for your student at the beginning of the course.

LETTER GRADES TO NUMERICAL SCORES

Dear **Jonas:**

I read your answer to "Inquiring Instructor" a couple of weeks ago about how to help our students who are struggling. I also gave my mid-term exam to my first year this past week, and have another problem. The mean score on the exam was a 51, which is lower than I'd like to see, but I feel that I graded it fairly. One of my colleagues said that it's just that the student quality has gone down over the years. Anyway, students were clearly upset by their scores, even the ones who had done well relative to the mean. All of them were asking to what letter grade (A, B, C, etc.) their numerical scores corresponded. I told them that I really don't set grade ranges until the end of the quarter and that the exam difficulty would be taken into account then. While they nodded politely I still sensed a high degree of anxiety among the students. What can I do?

Grappling Grader

Dear **Grappling Grader**:

In this situation I sometimes wonder if students' high school preparation is inadequate. As measured by SATs and high school GPAs, the quality of the first-year students has never been better: While their preparation for your specific course may vary, the numbers point to better quality students on average.

With regard to your exam, I would ask myself if the exam was well-designed. I always give exams that I intend to be well designed and fair, but sometimes, in retrospect, I have to acknowledge misjudgment. While you may have graded them fairly, you might reflect on how it compares to other exams you've given. You could do a question-by-question breakdown to see if there are any questions that students, including the best in your class, uniformly botched. This could be the sign of an ambiguously worded or overly difficult question. Was the level of analytical thought required on the exam beyond that required in homework? Was there enough time for the students to both think and work the exam?

The process by which an instructor assigns letter grades to numerical scores is obviously the prerogative of that instructor. But unnecessary anxiety among students about where they stand grade-wise in a class, can cut into their motivation to learn. Anxiety can also demoralize them to a point where they might withdraw from a course because they've misinterpreted their current grade status, i.e., they think they're doing poorly when in fact they are doing reasonably well compared to their peers. For example, a student who got a 61 on your mid-term might think this corresponds to a D or D- (from a high school frame of reference). So, should you assign a letter grade to these scores? And if so, how? The answer to the first question, in my opinion, is yes. My experience indicates that students put in more effort and perform better when I clearly communicate how they are doing in my class through the assignment of letter grades after each exam. Throughout high school, letter grades were assigned to numerical scores, and they expect the same at college. Furthermore, in high school, the grade cut-offs were fairly conventional, e.g., 90-100 = A, 80-90 = B, and so on. To go back to the earlier example, if a student got a 61 on your exam, that would be a D- or even an F but it probably isn't that low a grade on your mid-term.

Whatever system you use, it's important to communicate clearly the letter grades to which student scores correspond. Students carrying a demanding course load, have many anxieties about their academic performance, and are used to a more standard grading scheme, this is essential. Clear communication will motivate them to improve on their performance and keep them from misunderstanding how they're doing in your class.

Jonas

> **Quick Tip:** To build rapport with your class, let them know that while you are there as their coach, you must maintain levels of quality assurance. You can reassure them that it is not your intention to fail all students in the class, rather that you are there to instruct and encourage them to learn the material so they will earn the best grade possible.

IMPACT OF LATE GRADES

Dear **Jonas,**

Perhaps you can help us help our students. As department chair, I'd like to find a way to let faculty know how important it is to submit final grades on time. If grades are late, we are really hamstrung in our ability to assess our students' progress and communicate appropriately with them. Most faculty teaching are aware of our mid-term progress report system in which faculty identify students who perform below a satisfactory level of achievement and report them to our Student Services Office. These students are then contacted and provided with advice and counseling. Our office provides a similar review for every engineering freshman at the end of each term, and on-time final grades are absolutely critical for assessing students' overall progress.

We pride ourselves on sending each of our freshmen students an individualized letter summarizing his/her academic progress and level of achievement by the end of the week after finals, right after grades are due. We try to set our students up for success by providing the best counseling we can in a timely fashion. For example, the letter requires students who have failed or withdrawn from a course (or have encountered other academic trouble) to meet with his or her contact person in our Student Services Office to discuss problems encountered, to identify causes and to formulate solutions prior to the start of the next term. If a freshman has failed a prerequisite course, his or her schedule is modified accordingly so everything will be set for the beginning of the next term. As you might imagine our worst nightmare is encountering a missing grade - we don't know whether to congratulate the student, require a meeting, or change his schedule. All progress stops, and we are put in the uncomfortable and difficult position of chasing the instructor and getting a copy of the grades, recalculating QPA's, etc. Perhaps you can help us get the word out about the importance of submitting final grades on time.

Stood Up in Student Services

Dear **Stood Up**,

Wow! What a team effort! And, what a strong case for submission of grades on time! I have little to add to your eloquent plea, and I realize that sometimes a valiant faculty effort is required to meet tight deadlines (especially for late finals). However, the efforts of you and your colleagues in Student Services to set students up for success are no less valiant. I can only urge my academic colleagues to get those grades in on time so you can continue to provide accurate and timely counseling.

Jonas

Quick Tip: To help facilitate grading, prepare the answer key or scoring guide with assigned points before administering the exam. This allows any mistakes to be caught, and uses time effectively if there is little time between the exam and the due date for grades.

INCONSISTENT TEST PERFORMANCE

Dear **Jonas:**

There's a student in my class who seems to understand the material I'm teaching, attends all the classes, sits near the front of the room, correctly answers my questions, has done quite well on all of her homework but has failed both my exams! She can't be just copying the homework because she does grasp the concepts. What could be going on?

Mystified

Dear **Mystified**:

This is not unusual. There are several reasons that a student could be doing well in class and on homework, and yet have difficulty on tests. One, as you suggested, could be that she is not doing her own homework, but that seems unlikely in this case. Perhaps she doesn't really know how to prepare for a test. For instance does she actually work through new problems without looking at the solutions or just review previously solved ones? Does she simulate exam conditions and time herself to make sure she can work quickly enough?

Perhaps her problem is not with preparation but with test-taking techniques. You may be able to get a sense of this by looking at her exam. Does she seem to get stuck on one of the early problems, for example, and spend all her time on that one, rather than moving on and answering the questions she does know first? You might spend some time in classes giving suggestions on how to actually "attack" an exam.

Another possibility is that she suffers from test anxiety. Does she say she freezes or that her mind goes blank, even though she has studied and feels she knows that material? The on-campus Center for Counseling and Student Development offers workshops on dealing with test anxiety. Their staff is also available for consultation with faculty.

She may have a learning disability. Learning disabilities in the classroom is a very complex subject. If you think that may be the case, you can contact the on-campus Center for Disability Resources for information on how to effectively teach, assess the knowledge of and advise students with LD.

The first thing you should do is make an appointment with the student. Ask her to work on one of the problems from the exam (which she did incorrectly) in front of you. While she is working, encourage her to describe her reasoning out loud. By listening to how she thinks and what she looks for in the problem, you can get a sense of how well she understands the material and what is being asked of her, as well as obstacles she may be facing. Once those are addressed, you may have one more top student in your class!

Jonas

QuickTip: Contact Student Services or academic advisors for questions about student performance. Other people may be able provide additional insight for a particular student, and can also help to direct the student to additional services.

Chalk Talk – E-advice from Jonas Chalk

Chapter 9

Dear Jonas:

How Do I Get (and Keep) My TA's on Board?

Miriam Rosalyn Diamond

Faculty take on many roles when they teach including instructor, information provider, mentor, evaluator, tutor and facilitator. Another role to add to this list may be that of supervisor. Professors are frequently assigned teaching assistants (TA's) to help run their courses. Often graduate student TA's may be handpicked by the Professor (for instance, they may be students who excelled in that particular course during previous terms), or assigned by department administrators. Funding is provided to support the TA's studies, a single course may have one TA allotted to work for 10 hours weekly, or more than 12 TA's assigned for 20 hours each.

There are several challenges involved in overseeing the work of TA's. Probably one of the most important, and the one faculty are least prepared for, is that of manager. Expertise in management requires training and considerable experience, which not all professors have. Effective supervision entails the ability to articulate expectations clearly, maintain open lines of communication in many directions, provide clear expectations and correction on performance as needed, as well as offer support and recognition for quality work. There may also be the opportunity to guide teaching assistants in ways to juggle teaching along with their other responsibilities, such as conducting research and taking their own classes.

Teaching Assistants, as well, are not always prepared to take on their roles. They may need guidance on acting responsibly, as in returning graded homework on time and attending planning meetings. They also may require direction on ways of preparing to teach – whether in the classroom, laboratory or during office hours. Their skill and confidence may be low in both public and interpersonal communication. They may be unclear about what constitutes an appropriate relationship with their students, and may not know how to make referrals to other campus offices (such as counseling and disability services) as needed. They may also need to seek assistance in understanding the mechanics of fair grading (Diamond, 2002).

In addition, TA's vary greatly in their motivation to assume this role. Their level of interest in a teaching career may correlate with the amount of time and effort they are willing to devote to this assignment. By definition, graduate students have many other major demands on their time and energy, including their own classes and research. They may also be directly counseled by advisors and mentors not to expend too much time or effort carrying-out their TA assignment. Of course, some individuals are intrinsically motivated to excel in every task they assume, and will demonstrate dedication regardless of the circumstances under which they teach.

It is crucial that faculty make the effort to foster productive working relationships with their teaching assistants. This is an on-going process that begins before the start of classes and continues throughout the term. A good place to begin is by determining the level of teaching experience, and familiarity with the subject material, each TA has. This will inform the amount of initial training and ongoing supervision each TA will need so that both parties can feel comfortable about the quality of his/her work (Nyquist and Wulff, 1996).

An intensive pre-semester training program will enhance the success of all TA's, particularly those just arriving from other countries. These programs often include training in expressive and receptive communication, discussions about norms and expectations in the classroom, and opportunities for the TA's to conduct sample presentations to peers for feedback (Andrews, 1985).

Motivating TA's is also vital. It is important that faculty convey the significance of their assignment to the students, as well the department and university. TA's should be aware that even seemingly minor tasks, such as grading homework assignments, are not to be taken lightly (Nyquist and Wulff, 1996).

Throughout the term, multi-direction communication is key in promoting the effective training and performance of TA's. It also increases the likelihood of a smooth-running class. A survey of TA's and course administrators revealed that the majority of respondents in both groups felt TA's should be given more input in the formulation of class policies and decisions (Wilson and Stearns, 1985). However, fewer than half of those questioned saw how this could be implemented. The researchers suggested that faculty should ask questions and make a point to listen to their TA's. Discussions about decision-making processes and rationales will result in increased teaching staff competence and success.

Mentoring of TA's is especially effective when it includes discussions about their teaching goals, as well as the techniques they use to assess success. They can be encouraged to articulate the content and processes involved in each lesson they prepare. This includes an exploration and conscious selection of the styles TA's can take when teaching, such as serving as a provider of information, demonstrator, interpreter, coach, inquisitor, and motivator. In addition, faculty can encourage TA's to examine their expectations of students and the ways in which these expectations are conveyed (Andrews, 1985).

Another important component of TA supervision is performance evaluation and on-going feedback during the term. This can take the form of laboratory or class observations, mid-term surveys of students, and videotapes of the TA in action. In follow-up meetings, the faculty supervisor should address strength areas as well as suggestions for improvement. They can collaborate with the TA to develop goals and action plans in response (Davis, 1993, Nyquist and Wulff, 1996).

Jonas responded to many issues that arose when supervising teaching assistants. These include guiding TA's on their duties, dealing with TA's who appear to be shirking their responsibilities, and addressing TA's who haven't mastered the material they're expected to teach. Other concerns included how to coordinate multiple graders, developing a sense of teamwork, and supporting international TA's who are not yet fluent in English.

FURTHER READING

BOOKS

1. Andrews. J. D. W.,ed. (1985) Strengthening the Teaching Assistant Faculty. *New Directions for Teaching and Learning*. 22. San Francisco: Jossey-Bass, Inc.

2. Davis, B. G. (1993) *Guiding, Training, and Supervising Graduate Student Instructors. In Tools for Teaching.* San Francisco: Jossey-Bass, Inc. 384 – 390.

3. Diamond, M. R. (2002) *Preparing TAs to Respond to Ethical Dilemmas.* In W. Davis, (ed.) Ready to Teach: Graduate Teaching Assistants Prepare for Today and Tomorrow. Stillwater, OK: New Forums Press Inc. 47-50.

4. Marincovich, M. , Prostko, J. and Stout, F. , ed.s (1998) *The Professional Development of Graduate Teaching Assistants.* Bolton, MA: Anker Publishing Company, Inc.

5. Nyquist, J. D., and Wulff, D.H. (1996), *Working Effectively with Graduate Assistants.* Thousand Oaks, CA : Sage Publications.

6. Svinicki, M. (1994) The Teaching Assistantship: *A Preparation for Multiple Roles.* In W. J. McKeachie (ed.) Teaching Tips. Lexington, MA: DC Heath and Company. 230-249.

Articles

1. Wilson T. and Stearns J. (1985) *Improving the Working Relationship Between Professor and TA.* In J. D. W. Andrews (ed.) Strengthening the Teaching Assistant Faculty. Strengthening the Teaching Assistant Faculty. New Directions for Teaching and Learning. 22. San Francisco: Jossey-Bass, Inc. 35- 45.

2. Breslow, L. , *Working With TAs: Supervising TAs Calls for Faculty to be Managers, Team Leaders, Role Models, and Mentors.* MIT Teach Talk, XI, (2), November/December 1998. Available at: http://web.mit.edu/tll/published/tas.htm

Websites

1. How to Mentor Graduate Students: A guide for Faculty at a Diverse University. University of Michigan, Rackham Graduate School. Available at: http://www.rackham.umich.edu/StudentInfo/Publications/FacultyMentoring/contents.html

2. Rishel, T., A Handbook for Mathematics Teaching Assistants (Preliminary Edition) Cornell University & The Mathematical Association of America. http://www.maa.org/pfdev/tahandbook.html

3.   Showalter, E. The Risks of Good Teaching: How 1 Professor and 9 T.A.'s Plunged into Pedagogy. The Chronicle of Higher Education. July 9, 1999. http://chronicle.com

4.   Smith, K., Managing and Mentoring Graduate Teaching Assistants at The University of Georgia. http://www.isd.uga.edu/teaching_assistant/m&mbrochure.pdf or http://www.isd.uga.edu/teaching_assistant/index.html#12

5.   Sorenson, D.L. Johnson, T.D. Graham, S.T. QATA — Questions and Answers for Teaching Assistants. In Teaching and Learning. Brigham Young University. lrfr.html" http://www.byu.edu/fc/pages/tchlrfr.html

GUIDING TA'S

Dear **Jonas**:

Now that I've gotten my students on the right page about my expectations, I want to make sure that things go smoothly with my Teaching Assistants. Sometimes I get TA's who jump right in and do what they have to in terms of grading, supervising labs, holding review sessions and/or office hours and do it well. This term, I have a new crop of TA's who seem uncertain about what they should do. How can I show them how to grade, gauge when they should hold review sessions (and how to review material), and what their role is in the lab without ending up doing it all myself?

King of the Hill

Dear **King**:

Many graduate students come from undergraduate programs that didn't hire TA's, so they are unclear about their role and duties. Also, expectations vary from course to course and instructor to instructor. It is important that you meet with your TA's early in the term to outline your expectations of them. Be upfront about your expectations for their attendance in lectures, proctoring of exams, and holding tutoring as well as grading sessions. Provide guidelines on how quickly they should return problem sets and lab reports, the criteria you want them to use in grading, and the ways in which they should record student marks. Let them know how proactive you want them to be in lab and the way they should use the time in recitation sections. Outline the type of feedback about individual or group performance that you would like to receive and when. Talk about office hours - how many should they hold and the best way for them to utilize this resource to benefit students. Include discussions about what to do if a student is missing a lot of classes, ignoring safety regulations in

---

the lab, in danger of failing the course, or if the TA suspects academic dishonesty.

It's a good idea to invite TA's who successfully worked with this course in the past to talk with new TA's about the finer points in managing their end of the class. You may even want to set up a mentoring program, whereby successful veteran TA's are available to answer common questions throughout the term and provide triage so that the most sensitive and urgent issues go directly to you. Set up a regular meeting time with your TA's throughout the term. Some faculty meet with their assistants weekly or semi-monthly, while others hold meetings just before and after exams. It's also a good idea to meet with each TA individually no later than after the first month to give feedback on how well they are performing their duties and further clarify their responsibilities.

Some professors have an outline to guide their discussions with TA's. Professor Beverly Jaeger of the College of Engineering developed the form provided at the end of this column, to address responsibilities and provide feedback. You may want to use something similar.

Another helpful resource is the Center for Effective University Teaching. This office conducts university-wide TA orientations and workshops (on topics like collecting midterm feedback, understanding your students, and holding effective office hours) throughout the year. For more information, you and your TA's can turn to the TA Homepage.

Jonas

> **Quick Tip:** Encourage your TA's to keep you informed of common errors they find students making in problem sets and exams. This is useful feedback to you about topics that are worth clarifying in your lectures.

Teaching Assistant/Grader Expectations and Evaluation

TA Name:_____ Term:_____

TA e-mail:_____ Professor:_____

TA Office:_____ Course Name:_____

TA Office Hours:_____ Course Number:_____

TA Office Phone:_____ TA Home Phone_____

#	TA Duties	Expectation	Evaluation
1	Attend Lectures		N/A 1 2 3 4 5
2	Attend Labs, prepared to assist		N/A 1 2 3 4 5
3	Grade Homework/Labs/Projects		N/A 1 2 3 4 5
4	Meet regularly with Instructor		N/A 1 2 3 4 5
5	Post & Hold office/help hours		N/A 1 2 3 4 5
6	Conduct lab or help session(s)		N/A 1 2 3 4 5
7	Generate grade roster, SW: ____		N/A 1 2 3 4 5
8	Enter and maintain grade records		N/A 1 2 3 4 5
9	Assigned hours of responsibility		
Notes:			
	TA Conduct		
1	Demeanor: positive, respectful		N/A 1 2 3 4 5
2	Communication with Professor		N/A 1 2 3 4 5
3	Communication with students		N/A 1 2 3 4 5
4	Reliability, punctuality		N/A 1 2 3 4 5
5	Preparation		N/A 1 2 3 4 5
6	Attendance		N/A 1 2 3 4 5
Notes:			
	Quality of Grading		
1	Promptness		N/A 1 2 3 4 5
2	Thoroughness		N/A 1 2 3 4 5
3	Consistency with instructions		N/A 1 2 3 4 5
4	Checking for academic dishonesty		N/A 1 2 3 4 5
5	Reporting on unusual grades, work styles or results		N/A 1 2 3 4 5
Notes:			
Overall Evaluation of TA:			

Evaluation Scheme: N/A = Not Applicable   1 = Unacceptable 2 = Poor 3= Acceptable   4 = Good 5= Outstanding

Date of Preview: _____ Date of Review: _____

Initials: _____ Initials:_____

STANDARDS FOR MULTIPLE GRADERS

Dear Jonas:

I have two Teaching Assistants assigned to my course. One of their prime responsibilities is to grade lab reports. Last week – after the first reports were returned – a few of the students came to my office. They complained that the grading was unfair, and that the TA who graded took off complete credit for a computational error, while the other TA deducted only a couple of points and gave most of the credit if everything else was correct. I told the students I appreciate their concern and would look into it. Now what do I do?

Making the Grade

Dear Making the Grade,

It is critical that, in classes with multiple graders, marking is calibrated just to avoid this kind of situation. Before grading exams, lab reports or problem sets, it is important that you meet with TA's to work out clear guidelines for grading. You may want to provide sample work completed by former students to show how you would like points assigned.

Before papers are returned to students, it's a good idea to hold a follow-up session whereby the TA's can show each other (and you) how they marked various responses. (You could indicate that their initial marking be done in pencil, as it may be altered after discussion.) For my classes, I have them bring in an example of a top or perfect response, a representative poor response, and a rather typical middle-of-the-pool answer. They can share with you and each other how many points they gave to each. They should also be encouraged to bring in items where they had questions on how to grade. You can then provide direction, and help determine the grade. This also sets a model for the TA's to work collaboratively.

Once this system is in place, it should eliminate the need for you to review all grades throughout the term. It also provides a system for them to ask with each other if they have questions, and to check each other's calculations.

Another way to mark exams is to have one TA assigned to the same question for all students. That way, each item is graded uniformly. Of course, you should still meet with them ahead of time to make sure they are clear when to give partial credit, and how much.

It is also important that you have a clear grade appeal process in place by which grades can be reviewed and, if deemed appropriate, changed. Both TA's and students should understand the details of this procedure. Of course, it should be designed to minimize the likelihood of academic dishonesty, and in such a way that students aren't encouraged to take advantage of the system to gain points unfairly.

In any case, make it clear that TA's can check in with you whenever they have questions on evaluating student work.

Jonas

Quick Tip: Before the first lab reports are due, give TA's samples of well-written reports from prior years to enable them to guide students on preparing their own.

COMMUNICATION ABOUT GRADING

Dear **Jonas:**

Yesterday I received a call from an irate parent. His son is in my freshman lecture course (enrollment = 200), and failed the first two quizzes of the course. Apparently, if he fails my course, it jeopardizes his scholarship.

Since my TA's do the grading, I had no knowledge of the student or his status. I promptly called them into my office, and found out that this student has not yet handed in any problem sets, and earned 10 and 18 points (out of 100, where the means were in the 63 and 72) on each of the two quizzes. It turns out that there are about a dozen students in similar situations. I asked the TA's what they did about it, and they responded that they thought their only obligation was to grade and return the tests, let students know their office hours, and remind them of the deadline to drop classes.

Before the course started, I met with the TA's and told them to inform me if anything comes up I should know about during the term. Neither one told me about students in danger of failing. How can I get through to them that it's their responsibility to let me know about students in trouble, so I can be aware of what's going on in the class?

Out of the Loop

Dear **Out of the Loop,**

For many teaching assistants, this is their first job involving administrative duties. They may not be aware of what constitutes a situation they should bring to your attention. They need guidelines.

It sounds like you started the process in your initial meeting, encouraging them to approach you with any concerns. However, it is important to clarify *what kinds* of issues you want to be kept apprised of. You may want to give concrete examples (for example, failing students, students not completing most of their assignments, suspicions of academic dishonesty). You may want to explain the reason you want this information (e.g., to work with TA's to address situations early in the game, as well as to be able to provide informed responses to parental inquiries and contacts from the students' home departments).

You mentioned your initial meeting with the TA's. However, it was not clear whether you hold regular weekly or bi-weekly meetings with them throughout the term. This is a great way to keep the lines of communication open and keep on top of what's going on in your class.

Jonas

Quick Tip: Prior to the start of the term, provide your TA's with a written list of crucial dates when they are going to be most needed for running review sessions, holding extra office hours and grading, so they can make their vacation and travel arrangements with these in mind.

COMMAND OF COURSE MATERIAL

Dear **Jonas:**

I just collected mid-term feedback on my class. It turns out that students are frustrated with the fact that the TA's often do not know how to solve specific problems, or that they provide advice that is contrary to what I have taught. I don't have the time to provide remedial training for TA's on the class material, but I don't want a misinformed class. What to do?

Seeking Damage Control

Dear **Seeking:**

Sometimes Teaching Assistants are assigned to classes that they didn't take as undergraduates, or that address different course topics. In some situations, they've seen the material before, but never truly mastered it. It is important that you encourage them to take the responsibility to find out what they don't know and learn it BEFORE it comes up in class.

To address this problem, I give the TA's additional resource material to read and prepare ahead of time. I make it clear that I expect them to stay ahead of the students in terms of knowing and understanding the material. I also watch them carefully (sometimes even sitting in on parts of their recitation sections) and tell the TA's to talk with me if they are unsure about an operation or concept. (I'd much prefer to spend some time reviewing information with my TA's than having to backtrack in my classes with large numbers of confused students.) I also make it clear that they are expected to attend course lectures.

TA's are often afraid to admit to students when they don't have answers, as they think it undermines their effectiveness and authority. The truth is that the reverse is actually the case! You can help TA's understand that it is better to tell students, "I'll have to look that up (or work it out) and get back to you," when asked a question, than to give an answer of which they are unsure. You could model this, by describing a time when you had to do that, yourself. Also, if they find they said something incorrectly, direct them to provide accurate information to their students ASAP.

In the future, if you have any control over what TA's are appointed to work in your class, you might want to focus on selecting those with the specific educational background necessary for success with your class. If someone else does the assigning, it's a good idea to communicate with that person early in the process. Make them aware of what they should be looking for when placing someone in your class.

Jonas

> **Quick Tip**: Provide TA's with course syllabi, copies of textbooks, and sample exams a few weeks prior to the start of class with the expectation that they will "brush up" on the material.

SHIRKING RESPONSIBILITIES

Dear **Jonas**:

I'm having problems with the TA for my course. First, it turns out that he graded and returned the first round of papers without keeping a record of the grades. Then, he went to an out-of-state family reunion one week before the midterm, and was not available to run a timely review session. Due to an apparent glitch with the airlines, he returned several days later than expected, but communicated that to no one. For the second assignment, a few students have e-mailed and come to me complaining that he added up the points incorrectly on a number of papers. I see a disaster happening. What can I do?

The Road to Perturbation

Dear **Perturbed**,

It sounds like either your TA doesn't understand the obligations of his job, or that he is unmotivated to carry them out. I suggest you meet with him ASAP to determine which is the case.

Often, TA's are at the very beginning of their careers and have never held professional positions. It is important that you provide coaching about job expectations, such as the fact that he needs to keep his supervisor informed when he has to be away. Make sure he knows that, unless he is dealing with an emergency (and you might want to give concrete examples of what that includes), he should ASK if the timing of his absence is ok with the rhythm of the course. Give him a list of critical times in the class when your are relying on him to run review sessions, grade, and perform other duties. Let him know if it is his responsibility to find coverage by other TA's if he can't be there.

Have you outlined your expectations for him regarding grading? Make sure he understands that you expect him to keep a record of student grades. If you provide him with a pre-formatted spreadsheet or grade-book, it may give him the structure and reminder he needs. You also might want to spend time clarifying grading rubrics, and emphasize the importance of re-checking his math before finalizing the grades.

Another issue could be that he is simply unmotivated to carryout his responsibilities. He may take his assignment for granted, and not realize that TA-ing is a job, not simply a source of funding. Clarify for him that he has to fulfill his part of the bargain in order to *earn* the funding that comes with the position.

Also, he should be informed that the skills one picks up from TA-ing (public speaking, training, coaching, evaluating performance) are assets in any profession. So, regardless of whether he is planning a career in academia, he should plan to get as much out of this opportunity as possible.

If none of the above interventions seems to make much difference, I suggest you check with your department to determine whether, after a warning and if things still don't improve, he can be terminated from his position.

Jonas

Quick Tip: Prior to the start of classes, give your TA's a written list of what is expected of them.

FOSTERING A TEAM MENTALITY

Dear **Jonas**:

I am very upset. I gave an exam last week, in which the mean was 62 and the standard deviation was 9. That's fairly typical for my classes. I just found out that one of the TA's has been telling her students that the exam was "too difficult" and that it was much too long for the time allotted. So the students went to our department chair and complained.

This is the third time I am teaching this class. It's true that I hold high standards. I want the students to be aware of what they know and what they have yet to learn – without sugarcoating my feedback to them. I believe that exams should be longer than the time needed, so that everyone feels challenged. I don't expect any of my students to complete the entire test in the time provided.

Having said that, I do some grade curving at the end; the class mean usually ends up being a B-. The issue I have isn't about exam construction, it's about the fact that the TA's complained to the students and created a dynamic where it's me against the students, and I'm "the bad guy", instead of a class where we are all working together to increase student understanding and knowledge.

Burning Ears

Dear **Burning Ears**:

It is frustrating when your teaching team doesn't function as such. It is very important that TA's know from the start that they are to come directly to you if they have questions about how the class is being taught or run. It is possible that your teaching philosophy differs from theirs. Or they may be so early in their careers, they are naive and don't understand the choices and variables involved in setting up testing, assessment and grading procedures. It is very likely that they may still identify with the role of the student, or want the students to like them, and therefore are quick to criticize the professor.

In any case, it was inappropriate for them to voice these sentiments to the students. They should be told this. If students complain about the length of the test, the TA's can give students pointers on studying for and strategies for taking your exams. They can also encourage students with complaints to come directly to you, either in person or through less direct methods such as e-mails. Alternatively, they can let the students know that they will pass their concerns on to you. However, they should not make negative comments about the class or how it is run to students.

The TA's can take action by cueing you that it might be a good time to explain your testing approach to the students in class. They can also let you know directly that they heard from the students and if they, too, are worried about the exam length. The information provided may cause you to try a new testing approach. If you are convinced that this method works best for you, it can be a great opportunity for you to explain to the TA's why you test that way, thereby increasing their awareness of issues involved in the test construction and administration process.

To prevent the likelihood that this will occur in future classes, I suggest that in your preliminary meeting with TA's, you impress upon them that they are hired as members of the professional teaching team. They represent the department to students and there are expectations on how they will carry out their responsibilities. Make it clear that they should take concerns about the administration and teaching of the course directly to you. As a member of the team, you can assure them that you will to listen and consider alternate responses to their concerns.

Jonas

Quick Tip: If you have four or more Teaching Assistants, designate one (who has prior experience with this class, if possible) as Head TA to ensure communication between the students, TA's and professor.

TA'S NOT YET FLUENT IN ENGLISH

Dear Jonas:

In my department, all first year grad students who do not have outside scholarship funding support themselves through TA-ships. Often this means that they have just arrived from other countries where English is not their first language. Sometimes I have had TA's whose spoken English is so limited, I cannot understand them myself. Students often complain to me that they can't understand the TA's. Also, the TA's may tell them what to do in a lab, rather than asking the students and encouraging them to think for themselves. What should I do?

Multi-Cultural Mentor

Dear **Mentor:**

Many faculty members express frustration in working with international teaching assistants (ITA's) who do not yet have a command of spoken English. It is critical to be aware that this process is frustrating for the ITA's, as well. In addition to meeting the usual demands of juggling their TA duties and their own course loads/research, they often have to adjust to unfamiliar campus norms and cultures, as well as approaches to teaching and learning to which they are unaccustomed. It can also be difficult for them to understand their students (particularly colloquialisms), and they may find it challenging to make themselves understood. Acknowledging this from the start will establish a relationship where these issues can be openly discussed, rather than swept under the rug.

Spend some time acculturating your ITA's to the expectations and concerns of our students, explaining what behaviors are and are not acceptable in classes – as well as ways to handle the unacceptable behaviors. (For instance, in some countries, "sharing" answers on an exam is not considered cheating, while here it is considered academic dishonesty and needs to be directly addressed.) In addition, there are several techniques teaching assistants can use to convey information if their expressive skills in English are limited. For instance, they can use lots of demonstrations, props, and illustrations to supplement instruction. They can write key words on blackboard/overhead/PowerPoint, in case their pronunciation is unclear. Handouts prepared ahead of time can help students follow instruction.

They should be reminded to face students while speaking (in the case of blackboard work, they can write the information down first, then turn around and speak). It is important that they are encouraged to maintain eye contact with their class (which is not a norm in every culture). This will help them discern who looks confused, and will make it easier to be heard. Early in the course, they should acknowledge that English is not their first language, and for their students to let them know when they speak too quickly, quietly, or if students don't understand something. They should also check in with students periodically – e.g. " What can I clarify for you?" "What questions do you have?" (and wait at least 10 seconds while scanning the students' faces to make sure students have enough time to respond.)

A number of departments conduct programs called "microteaching" prior to the start of the term. This is useful for both international and North American educated TA's. Each is given a topic, sample problem or lab demonstration to conduct on before their peers. They are given at least one to two days' time to prepare a 5 - 10 minute lesson. Ideally, they will be assigned a mentor or experienced TA who can help them plan and run-through the lesson before presenting it. The lesson is presented and videotaped. Following this, a section of the videotape is replayed, with the TA giving the first feedback on the strengths and areas for improvement on his/her own lesson. The others than also give a few pointers and reinforce strengths that they see, as well.

The TA should then get a second chance to present the lesson, incorporating many of the suggestions given and ideas gathered from feedback and by watching his/her peers in action. It is helpful if supervising faculty make a point to observe their TA's in action. Let them know you will be sitting on their recitation or lab, and decide with them which day and time will be best. During the observation, be supportive and don't interrupt his/her lesson (unless s/he gives misinformation or is having an extremely difficult time being understood). After the session, sit with each TA individually and discuss the strengths of his/her teaching, as well as suggestions for improvement. Approach this in an encouraging (not punitive) manner.

Microteaching and observation-feedback is useful in supporting the work of all TA's, not just those for whom English is a second language.

Having said all that, some TA's English is so limited, they may be better (and more comfortable) initially placed in roles where they are not directly instructing students on a regular basis. These roles include grading (as long as they can understand the work handed in and write clear comments in return), lab set-up, and technical course support (such as posting information on the web and preparing/driving audiovisual aspects of in-class presentations, such as overheads or PowerPoint).

Jonas

> **Quick Tip:** Provide a list of campus resources for your TA's, including contact information for tutoring centers, offices in support of students with disabilities, and staff of the college counseling center,

as well as guidelines of how and when these offices can be of use.

Chapter 10

Dear Jonas:

How Can I Use Your Information to Help my Faculty?

Miriam Rosalyn Diamond

There are several roles Jonas played in faculty development function of the GE Master Teaching Team. One of the most important was developing community among faculty from diverse departments and colleges. Another important role was the discourse and development Jonas promoted among the GE instructional team members. Finally, Jonas served as a vehicle to increase the insight and teaching repertoire of faculty across the campus.

Community is not a term that immediately comes to mind when many people hear the word "faculty". Independence and self-reliance are often considered the hallmarks of academicians. Courses are usually created and taught by one person. In many disciplines, research performed independently is granted more weight than collaborative studies. Even work schedules may vary greatly among members of the same department.

One of the biggest hurdles facing faculty is "creating enduring relationships with colleagues" (Bode, 1999, p.118). Professional partnerships may develop as a result of building such connections. Individuals may also benefit by broadening their perspective and understanding how each person contributes to the bigger picture.

Boice (2000) takes the argument one step further, stating that new faculty who have positive interactions with their peers and develop support systems are more likely to succeed professionally than those who distance themselves.

Regarding the teaching role, Qualters (2000) considers ways to address the isolation that so often prevails in that activity. She finds that participating in group dialogues about the experience and exploring how and why we teach the way we do in a communal setting, increased confidence and professional development.

The Jonas Chalk e-columns provided an opportunity for faculty with the common goal of teaching engineering students, to be invited to come together as a community to celebrate, problem solve and get to know each other. Jonas was a means of communicating and publicizing programs for faculty who taught freshmen engineers. These were unique events, as the professors who received the e-mails represented several departments (mathematics, physics, chemistry, engineering) and two colleges (the College of Arts and Sciences, the College of Engineering). However, they had many students in common, and were delivering a common curriculum.

In an effort to become acquainted and promote communication between faculty in the various departments, we held quarterly luncheons. Some of these were structured to include ice-breakers, report presentations, and working sessions on teaching. Jonas provided a venue to announce these events.

In addition, the School of Engineering recognized the importance of effective instruction among faculty in Arts and Sciences. These professors played a central role in establishing a foundation of skill and knowledge upon which the Engineering faculty then built their courses. Therefore, awards were established for faculty in Physics, Math, and Chemistry by the Engineering Department to acknowledge and reward outstanding teaching of their students. Jonas was instrumental in announcing the winners, as well as issuing invitations to an awards reception.

Circles of Influence

In addition, the columns sometimes sparked electronic interchange about instruction among professors from different disciplines. In response to a column on how to avoid the pre-class onslaught by students, one faculty member e-mailed all column recipients his system of collecting assignments at the end, rather than the start, of class. Another reader e-mailed him voicing her concerns that this approach could increase the likelihood that students will skip class to complete their work. He responded that this had not occurred in his classes. Thus, Jonas was responsible for fostering discourse about teaching and building connections among strangers housed in distinct parts of the university

Another example occurred in a Jonas team meeting during the preparation of a column on the use of office hours, when the suggestion was raised to arrange a follow-up meeting with a struggling student. One Jonas member suggested removing that suggestion from the column, saying that it was unrealistic, and that he never would make a second appointment for students regarding the same difficulty. A coleague countered the remark, saying that she often asks students to return to her office a week or so later to check back about their progress. Thus, the suggestion was left in, and the first professor became aware of one more option to use in assisting students having difficulties with course material.

This kind of discourse took place electronically, as well. The person (or occasionally two people) who had the lead writing positions for drafting Jonas' response that week would e-mail the draft to all committee members. The rest of the

---

group then suggested edits, adding tactics they would use to address that concern, as well as suggesting removing or clarifying approaches that seemed inappropriate or vague. They might also add a literature reference to help faculty understand that the scholarship of teaching is grounded in research just like their disciplines. Figure 2 shows an example of one column-in-progress, complete with comments and suggested edits by team members.

This collaboration, both in electronic and face-to-face formats, provided faculty members a venue in which to raise common concerns, weigh various approaches, and share the steps they commonly take to deal with issues. It also provided the opportunity to learn about educational literature and research on the topics, as members of the teaching center contributed information on instructional research to the conversations. The value of these discussions was evident when, during a summer break, one team member wrote in an e-mail to his peers: "Just wanted to thank all of you for the friendship, humor, insights, advice, therapy…etc., during the past year. I genuinely looked forward to being with the group every week….and hope we can reconvene with new vigor in the fall. Someone cue Kumbaya for the group hug!" In fact, at the end of the grant cycle, the group voted to continue working on Jonas voluntarily, stating that it was the only time they could discuss teaching with colleagues and get to know faculty from other parts of the university. Furthermore, team members chose to devote one hour of their hectic schedules for weekly meeting finding the face-to-face discussions a valuable component of the process. They appreciated the fact that a concrete product resulted from the pooled experiences of the team, and most importantly, found the process fun!

Finally, the entire university benefited from the development of this resource. Jonas columns were archived, listed by topic and posted on Northeastern's GE Master Teachers web page. This page has a link from the teaching center's website, so all faculty can access it. In addition, the column is reprinted quarterly in *Teaching Matters,* the teaching center's faculty newsletter.

What are the implications for faculty development? First, the success of this program lay in the fact that Jonas was written *by faculty for faculty.* The writers knew the current issues and struggles occurring in (and out of) the classroom at that university. They understood what responses were realistic and what actions most professors were unlikely to take. It was written in an accessible, collegial format with Jonas often talking about his struggles as well.

Second, team members themselves gained in knowledge and experience as a result of participating in the discourse and debate that took place while collaborating to create a weekly product. We also created cross-disciplinary and cross-college connections that improved overall communication and collaboration.

Third, as this was delivered in an electronic format, a resource on effective teaching was collected and made accessible for the entire university, using new technologies. When a concern arose, faculty could turn to the electronic list of Jonas columns and quickly get some direction and ideas about how to handle the issue. Those who felt they lacked the time to attend workshops, were reluctant to contact teaching center staff, or seek outside guidance on a particular area, found the Jonas web page an easy venue in which to get sound advice. This was readily available to adjunct professors, instructors at satellite sites and teaching assistants, as well.

Considerations in Developing an Advice E-column for Faculty

The team generating responses will be most effective, and profit most from the process, if they are selected from several different areas and disciplines within the university.

They need not all be award-winning faculty, as long as they are serious about promoting effective teaching. The committee should have a clear mission and know their target population. Offering incentives and/or rewards to participants will sustain their continued efforts.

Questions can be recruited from members of the faculty at teaching workshops, meetings, and retreats. It has been our experience that faculty are more likely to submit questions given the opportunity at such gatherings, rather than to respond to general requests via mass e-mail or mailings.

Each question or topic should be assigned to a specific team member designated to prepare the initial draft. The lead writer should also read one or two articles on the topic so as to incorporate scholarship as well as personal experience into the text of the column. The format of an original question may need editing to maintain confidentiality about sensitive issues. Another question may require some elaboration to adequately describe the particular situation.

Once the question is clarified and the first draft of the reply composed, the column can be circulated within the team for comments, additions and questions. It is important to establish a respectful, constructive approach to discussing and refining the columns. Members should feel free to ask for clarification, add their pointers, and voice concern about the wording of specific items.

Final copies can be distributed via e-mail, publications, faculty dining hall bulletin boards, or on websites.

It is also important to find a way to get feedback from the target audience. Are they reading the columns? Do they find the topics relevant? Are the suggestions helpful? Surveys can be taken at programs and meetings, with the process revised in response.

The simple, cost-effective process of a collaboratively driven advice column can be an accessible resource to support the work of faculty on many levels. Through building community, creating a forum for discourse, and serving as a resource using technology, e-advice can promote timely and effective teaching.

Figure 2: Sample Jonas in Progress

Dear Jonas:

Recently, a first-year engineering student who had been absent for one of my classes came to my office hours to tell me that it was because of ~~a~~ a ~~mandatory practice that her coach had scheduled~~ special conference tournament her team had played in. She's on the women's basketball team, and this ~~extra practice was called after they had lost a game the night before~~ tournament was a post-season event. As a result, she had missed an important review for the ~~mid-term~~ final, and she's already struggling. **Majoring in engineering requires a lot of time and effort. I feel that students in this field need to make a choice – either their academics come first, or they should re-consider their major.** I suggested that perhaps she couldn't be an engineer and a varsity athlete. She seemed very upset when I said this. ~~What else could I have said to her?~~ What are my responsibilities in this case? I find it frustrating that I'm supposed to help her when she misses class like this.

A Lacking Sports Sympathizer

Dear Lacking:

Although they're often ~~perceived~~ **mislabeled** as "dumb jocks," **the fact is that** ~~sFirst of all, believe it or not, s~~student athletes **regularly** succeed in a number of very challenging majors at our university, including engineering. In many cases, student-athletes have a higher graduation rate than non-athletes in their peer group. These students have to be extremely motivated to be both good in their academic pursuits and meet the

---

demands of whatever team they're on. They also have to be better-than-average time managers-, ~~to~~ juggl~~ing~~ing classes, labs, and recitations with practices, team meetings and travel to away games.

However, like most first year students, student-athletes are learning how to manage their time without the help of parents, and with the additional responsibilities that come with living away from home (for example, getting up on time, doing their laundry, etc.). In addition to these pressures, it is likely that student-athletes who are on a scholarship perceive~~see~~ their athlete status as the only way they can afford to ~~financially for them to stay~~ go to~~in~~ school. A similar kind of pressure exists for students who have to work a lot of hours to support themselves while attending school ~~(let's call them student employees)~~. All of this is a lot ~~to put~~of pressure for ~~on~~ an 18 or 19 year-old.

~~So, what could you have done differently in this situation?~~ According to ~~the Northeastern's~~ our student handbook (p. 10), students are allowed to miss class for an intercollegiate athletic event, and faculty are required to provide assistance in making up for that class. However, the student should learn from this experience. If this situation were to occur again, ~~It's not so much what you could have done, but what you need to encourage the student to do, particularly if this extra practice type of situation ever comes up again. It's important that we help our students to become better, more responsible decision-makers, and not simply victims of their circumstances. As soon as she found out about the extra practice~~, she should ~~have~~ e-mailed or called all of the professors whose classes ~~were~~are impacted by th~~is~~e athletic event, and explained the situation. This can reduce misunderstanding between faculty members and the student. **If she had done this** ~~f~~~~for your class, this could have resulted in scheduling a meeting between you and the student to go over the material~~. Additionally she could have arranged to get the notes for the class from another student or two, gone over them and then met with you with any questions.

Since the student is struggling in your class, you could have talked ~~to~~ **with** her about her study habits. Ask about the amount of time she is putting into your class assignments, quiz and exam preparation, etc. Is she working in a study group, or trying to go it alone? Does she know about the tutors who are there to help with first year engineering courses**? Has she sought help from the support services for student athletes?.** These are all worthwhile questions to ask not only this student, but all students who come to you because they're struggling. Again, it's important for ~~them~~ students to learn **that** ~~they need~~ **success is facilitated if they identify problems early,** to make **appropriate** decisions and take **timely** action to resolve ~~their~~ **these** problems. The University, College of Engineering, and in many cases, your department have a number of resources to help students. We ~~need to~~ **should** encourage ~~them~~ students to use those resources when they need help.

~~Ultimately, as a last resort, when you have a student athlete or student employee whose other time commitments seem to be impacting their schoolwork, you could have a discussion with that student about making choices. Again, it's not your job to tell them which decision to make. But you can talk about the importance of doing well in their academics versus staying on an athletic team or working many hours at a job. If it's an issue of financial aid, they should see their financial aid counselor, who can sometimes find additional funds to help out. Again, we've provided a lot of support mechanisms; we need to encourage students to seek them out as responsible decision makers.~~

Further Reading

Books:

1. Bode, R.K. (1999) *Mentoring and Collegiality*. In R.J. Menges (ed.) *Faculty in New Jobs*. San Francisco: Jossey-Bass, Inc. 118- 144.

2. Boice, R. (2000) *Advice for New Faculty Members*: Nihil Nimus. Needham Heights, MA: Allyn and Bacon.

Website:

1. Qualters, D. (2000) *Creating Faculty Community*. The National Teaching and Learning Forum. 9 (4). Available at: http://ctl.stanford.edu/teach/NTLF/v9n4/lrndiary.htm

ANNOUNCING AWARDS

Colleagues,

The Engineering College Dean has asked me to announce the recipients of the Outstanding Teachers of First Year Engineering Students Awards for 2002 and invite you all to the College of Engineering Awards Reception at 3 PM on June 4 to congratulate them and other College Award winners. I am pleased to congratulate:

- **Physics:** Professor _____
- **Mathematics:** Professor _____
- **Chemistry:** Professor _____
- **Engineering :** Professor _____

At the reception, all will receive Award Certificates and an honorarium of $1000. Please add your congratulations at the reception or when you see them. This year marks the second year that these awards will be presented. I hope to see you on the 4th.

Jonas

INVITATION TO LUNCH

Dear **Readers**,

I am writing to extend an invitation to all of you for our traditional Spring Term Kickoff Luncheon at the Faculty Center. The luncheon will be held on Thursday, March 28, during activities period. As in past quarters, this is an opportunity to share wisdom, woes, and some laughs with faculty in other departments who are teaching freshman engineering students. While there is no formal program for the luncheon, we encourage informal discussions on the myriad of issues related to teaching freshman.

We are interested in your views on the published

ChalkTalk columns, and again invite you to submit topics, issues or questions for future columns. Of course, you can always write to Jonas directly with your questions, concerns or with information on your own innovations in teaching. The ChalkTalk editors always welcome your input.

Please respond to this invitation whether you do or do not plan to attend on Thursday March 28 at 12:00 p.m. in the NU Faculty Center. The members of the GE Master Teaching Team look forward to seeing you there. Best wishes to you all for an enjoyable and productive Spring Break.

Jonas

Quick Tip: Get there early before the shrimp cocktail is gone! I know I missed it last time.

JONAS SIGNS OFF FOR THE SUMMER

Dear Readers,

Although the weekly question and answer emails will be taking a summer vacation, I won't be. Feel free to send along any questions or concerns that you may have. If *you* have a question or comment, others are likely to have it as well. Please don't hesitate to write - we will use your ideas for columns in the fall.

Just a reminder that the Center for Effective University Teaching staff will be available this summer if you have questions, would like your class video-taped, or would like midterm student feedback.

Best wishes to you all for a productive, restorative summer in teaching, research or other activities.

Jonas

> **Quick Tip:** If you're teaching a summer class or have a question as you prepare for the fall, feel free to check out the Jonas archives.

Chalk Talk – E-advice from Jonas Chalk